Entrepreneurship and Employment in the Caribbean Community

Entrepreneurship and Employment in the Caribbean Community:

Policies for Hydrocarbon-Rich Countries

By

Don Charles

Cambridge Scholars Publishing

Entrepreneurship and Employment in the Caribbean Community:
Policies for Hydrocarbon-Rich Countries

By Don Charles

This book first published 2023

Cambridge Scholars Publishing

Lady Stephenson Library, Newcastle upon Tyne, NE6 2PA, UK

British Library Cataloguing in Publication Data
A catalogue record for this book is available from the British Library

ISBN (10): 1-5275-0152-3
ISBN (13): 978-1-5275-0152-2

TABLE OF CONTENTS

Preface/ Abstract vii

Chapter One 1
Introduction
1.1 Background 1
1.1 Research Problem 3
1.2 Objective 4
1.3 Outline 4

Chapter Two 6
Literature Review of Successful Cases of Education and Entrepreneurship
2.1 Nigeria 7
2.2 Malaysia 8
2.3 Singapore 9
2.4 Summary Insight 13

Chapter Three 15
CARICOM Member States Labour Market Overview
3.1 Labour Statistics of T&T 18
3.2 Labour Statistics of Guyana 20
3.3 Labour Statistics of Suriname 22
3.4 Shifting Employment 23
3.5 Summary Insight 25

Chapter Four 27
Understanding Unemployment and Underemployment
4.1 Macroeconomic Shocks and Economy-Wide Problems 28
4.2 Lack of Experience of Young Workers and the Flawed Education System 31
4.3 Excess Supply of Skilled Labour 33
4.4 Inefficiency in Public Sector Hiring 37
4.5 Inefficiency in the On-the-Job Training Programme 43
4.6 Summary Insight 45

Chapter Five 46
Stakeholders and Required Institutional Framework for Employment Creation
5.1 The Government 46
5.2 Public Institutions 49
5.3 The Private Sector.. 52
5.4 Other Non-Government Actors.. 55
5.5 Implementation and Coordination Project Steering Committee ... 58
5.6 Summary Insight... 60

Chapter Six 62
Identifying Potential Sectors for Employment Creation
6.1 Export of Education 64
6.2 Creative Industries 67
6.3 Technical Vocational Services.. 69
6.4 Niche Industries 71
6.5 Export Professional Services 73
6.6 Summary Insight... 77

Chapter Seven... 79
Policy Recommendations to Encourage Entrepreneurship
7.1 Entrepreneurship and Business Incubation 79
7.2 Career Guidance and Entrepreneurship Education 87
7.3 E-commerce.. 90
7.4 Summary Insight... 94

Chapter Eight.. 96
General Conclusion

References 101

Appendix 111
A.0 Econometric (Empirical) Analysis of the Statistical impact of Services Upon Economic Output 111
A.1 Data.. 111
A.2 Methodology: Pretesting.. 112
A.3 Methodology: Regression 114
A.4 Methodology: Diagnostic Testing.. 115
A.5 Results... 116

PREFACE/ABSTRACT

Trinidad and Tobago (T&T), Guyana, and Suriname, are Caribbean Community (CARICOM) Member States that are fortunate to be endowed with commercial reserves of hydrocarbons. Hydrocarbon revenues acquired by the respective governments can be used to fund the cost of several merit goods, amongst which the most commendable is the expenditure on education.

Without a doubt, the subsidisation of tertiary education carries tremendous public benefits, the most notable are income improvement, and poverty reduction. However, at the end of the education programme, graduates will be looking for work. If a nationwide education programme is not complemented with a supporting employment creation programme a situation can arise where sufficient employment opportunities are not created for all the people. Furthermore, it is unrealistic to expect a government that is seeking to build the competitiveness of its nation to employ all its citizens.

This study's objectives are threefold. The first is to examine the labour market in the hydrocarbon-rich CARICOM Member States. The second is the review of successful case studies of entrepreneurship in countries similar circumstances to the Caribbean. The third is to provide policy recommendations to address this employment problem in the hydrocarbon-rich CARICOM Member States.

An analysis of the education and the labour market in the hydrocarbon-rich CARICOM Member States reveals several deficiencies. The education system in the countries were largely influenced by their colonial heritage. A large focus is placed on academics rather than what the labour market needs. This system produces several graduates with skills that have a weak demand. This in turn results in several graduates being required to be retrained to work in a job, as well as an excess supply of skilled labour. Employers are justified in asking for workers to acquire "work experience" as this seems to be the more appropriate way to procure workers with useful skills. Definitely, an education system that encourages people to train for over 15 years, but produces graduates that are still unprepared to work, is flawed. Indeed, there is an urgent need for education reform to ensure that young people develop the skills and competencies needed by the labour market.

The much desired policy recommendation is the promotion of entrepreneurship in the hydrocarbon-rich CARICOM Member States. While this can produce sustainable income for people, the countries' present culture does not promote entrepreneurship as a first choice. People are socialised to go to school, obtain passes, then look for a job rather than becoming an entrepreneur. Moreover, many citizens of the hydrocarbon-rich Member States are faced with obstacles that prevent them from becoming successful entrepreneurs on their own.

Policy efforts by the government would be required to break this culture and to create the correct enabling environment for entrepreneurship. The ideal entrepreneurship policy would consist of a comprehensive and holistic business incubation programme, which integrates business mentoring, with educational training, with start-up financing, and e-commerce. These are the factors that are mandatory for small and medium-scale entrepreneurs to achieve success. Once implemented properly, this can stimulate widespread entrepreneurship in the hydrocarbon-rich CARICOM Member States, and set the countries on the path to achieving sustainable inclusive growth.

CHAPTER ONE

INTRODUCTION

1.1 Background

In the Caribbean Community (CARICOM), 3 countries are known to possess commercial reserves of hydrocarbons. They include Trinidad and Tobago (T&T), Guyana, and Suriname. T&T has the oldest oil industry, which spans over a century (Boopsingh and McGuire 2014). Commercial reserves of oil were discovered in Guyana in 2015 by Exxon Mobil, and from 2020 the export of oil commenced from the country (Thomas 2020). In 1928 oil was first discovered in Suriname in the District of Nickerie, which is close to the border with Guyana (Griffith and Bihariesingh-Raghoenath 2016).

As T&T has the longest oil industry, it had the most time to spend its oil rents. These oil rents have been used to fund many public and merit goods, including infrastructure development, such as roads, schools, and hospitals; subsidise electricity costs, health care, public transportation, water utilities; and expand the social safety net through welfare programmes. The Government of the Republic of Trinidad and Tobago (GORTT) also used its oil rents to subsidise the cost of tertiary education. While the public expenditure on all the aforementioned public and merit goods brings some public benefit to society, the expenditure on tertiary education can be singled out as it has the potential to develop the capacity and productivity of labour.

The initial tertiary education subsidisation programme was titled "Dollar for Dollar" and it saw the GORTT cover 50% of the cost of tuition for tertiary education programmes for citizens of T&T pursuing this education in the country. The Cabinet of the GORTT agreed by Minute No. 229 dated January 22, 2004, to the establishment of the Government Assistance for Tuition Expenses (GATE) Programme (Hosein and Franklin 2010).

At its inception, GATE was a mere renaming of the Dollar for Dollar programme as it offered the subsidisation of 50% of the cost of tuition for tertiary education. Students that took a means test were subsidised with 100% of the cost of tuition. There were no official criteria for the means test, however, the objective of the means test was to provide an avenue for full funding of the cost of tuition for students from low-income households. On September 28, 2005, through the 2005-2006 budget, the GORTT made a historic announcement.

> *"Mr. Speaker, that with effect from January 1, 2006, all nationals of Trinidad and Tobago enrolled at public tertiary institutions, namely UWI, UTT, COSTAATT and other institutions where the Government sponsors students, will be eligible for free tuition, that is free public tertiary education"* (GORTT 2005, 15).

This simple announcement had vast and profound implications. Full subsidisation of tertiary education effectively made tertiary education accessible to all citizens of T&T. In fact, it was more than just an increase in access to education. There was market penetration, as a large number of citizens of T&T began to pursue tertiary education. This can be demonstrated by the increase in T&T's tertiary participation rate from 6.06% in 2000 (World Bank 2020), to 65.23% by 2015 (Simms et al. 2016).

Although there were problems with the administration of GATE, the programme is an effective tool in creating opportunities for people. However, at the end of an educational programme, people expect to go to work to earn an income. It is also a reasonable expectation for the citizens of T&T that benefited from the GATE programme to pursue employment opportunities in T&T.

Every year, thousands of citizens of T&T graduate from tertiary educational programmes operating in the country. For example, in 2019, the University of the West Indies (UWI) reported that approximately 4,000 degrees were awarded from the St. Augustine Campus (UWI 2019). UWI is only one of the many tertiary education intuitions in T&T. Other notable national intuitions include the University of Trinidad and Tobago (UTT), the College of Science, Technology and Applied Arts of Trinidad and Tobago (COSTATT), and the Cipriani College of Labour and Cooperative Studies. There are also multiple private tertiary educational institutions operating in the country which produce thousands of graduates. As the GATE programme was gradually expanded to include post-secondary education, every year several students graduate from the National Energy Skills Centre (NESC) and other technical vocational programmes with technical vocational skills. The number of these combined graduates can easily be approximately 10,000 people (Paul 2019).

Unfortunately, in T&T, 10,000 new jobs are not created every year. Although the government plays a lead role in employment creation either directly or indirectly, the government cannot provide a job for every single graduate. Even if in one given year, a government can provide jobs for all the graduates, the government will never be able to provide jobs for all graduates every year.

Although by the end of 2021 the Governments of Guyana and Suriname did not have a similar tertiary education programme in operation, it can be reasonable to expect them to pursue similar human capacity development after they enter their hydrocarbon boom and earn large oil rents. This is logical given that the tertiary enrolment in Guyana is 11.62%, and Suriname is 10.5%, and the windfall rents would be more than sufficient to subsidise tertiary education costs.

If Guyana and Suriname follow with similar tertiary education subsidisation, they could experience the same problem of excess supply of tertiary labour. This can result in unemployment, and underemployment.

An alternative option would be to look at the private sector in the respective hydrocarbon-rich CARICOM countries to create jobs. Unfortunately, the private sector is not in business to create employment opportunities. They are in business to earn a profit. The private sector will only hire labour if it allows them to produce output to help them earn their profit. But once the private sector operates on traditional microeconomic rules (equating the marginal cost (of labour) to marginal revenue), some people will be left behind.[1]

1.1 Research Problem

In T&T, every year thousands (approximately 10,000) of graduates are exiting tertiary educational institutions. However, 10,000 new jobs are not being created every year. In 2018 the total number of unemployed people was 24.9 thousand, and the unemployment rate was 3.9%. But due to a low

---

[1] Goal 8 of the Sustainable Development Goals (SDGs) is themed "Decent Work and Economic Growth". The goal seeks to encourage economic growth while envisaging full employment and decent work. Moreover, as the SDGs promote sustainability, they do not recommend that anyone is left behind.

labour force participation rate of 59.1%, 438.6 thousand willing able-bodied people of working age did not have work.

Likewise, in Guyana in 2017, the working-age population was 550,831 persons and the labour force participation rate was 56%, indicating that 242 thousand people were out of work. In Suriname, approximately 66,433 people, or 21.5% of the working-age population were without work in 2005.

Therefore, there is a need for a programme that can facilitate income-earning opportunities for the people without work in the hydrocarbon-rich CARICOM Member States.

1.2 Objective

The hydrocarbon-rich CARICOM Member States are faced with a problem where sufficient decent work is not being generated for its non-institutionalised working-age population. This study's objectives are threefold. The first is to examine the labour market in the hydrocarbon-rich CARICOM Member States. The second is to review successful case studies of entrepreneurship in countries similar circumstances to the Caribbean. The third is to provide policy recommendations to address this employment problem in the hydrocarbon-rich CARICOM Member States.

Solutions to this labour market problem extend beyond a single actor. This study also seeks to highlight the need for a much stronger and clearer vision of the national decision-makers in enhancing the institutional framework and strengthening partnerships to adequately connect the hydrocarbon-rich CARICOM Member States' education industry with its labour market.

1.3 Outline

This study is structured as follows. Chapter Two synthesizes the literature on various approaches to entrepreneurship in other countries similar circumstances to the Caribbean. Chapter Three provides an overview of the economy of the hydrocarbon-rich CARICOM Member States, as well as their labour markets. Chapter Four analyses the labour market problem. Chapter Five identifies the main stakeholders that would be responsible for triggering an employment transformation in each respective hydrocarbon-rich CARICOM Member State. Chapter Six highlights the sectors which can be targeted for employment creation by the respective governments. Chapter Seven explores the policy recommendations to stimulate an appropriate environment to generate employment in the hydrocarbon-rich

CARICOM Member States. Chapter Eight provides a general conclusion to this study.

CHAPTER TWO

LITERATURE REVIEW OF SUCCESSFUL CASES OF EDUCATION AND ENTREPRENEURSHIP

The root words of entrepreneurship are 'entreprende' and 'unternhmen', which mean to do something different (Cunningham and Lischeron 1991). Entrepreneurship in its earliest form can be traced to activities involving trade, the discovery of trade routes, and the desire to make a profit by the merchant class. Although early trade was characterised mainly by barter, people quickly learned that through the specialisation in a few select areas while trading the surplus output would allow all parties to experience the gains of trade. Specialisation and trade eventually gave rise to opportunities to increase individuals' prosperity. Eventually, as institutions were developed and as the monetary system replaced the barter system, entrepreneurship emerged as an avenue to grow wealth for the merchants, and the economic fortune of countries (Joseph and Nkuda 2021).

There is no one universally accepted definition of entrepreneurship or an entrepreneur. For instance, Schumpeter (1911) defined an entrepreneur as an individual who introduces new products and new services. Entrepreneurship in the Schumpeterian context required creative destruction, and the creation of a new product or service. This definition of an entrepreneur and entrepreneurship is aligned with innovation and invention. It requires the discovery of something new, which is later turned into a business opportunity.

Other authors held a more open perspective of entrepreneurship. For example, Stevenson (1983) defines entrepreneurship as the pursuit of opportunity without regard to resources currently controlled. Akinbode (2009) defines the entrepreneur as the man who perceives business opportunities and takes advantage of the scarce resources to use them profitably. While Thompson (1999) asserts that an entrepreneur is someone who can identify unexploited business opportunities.

The aforementioned definitions recognise that there may be a demand for a good or service in an economy and a business opportunity can arise if the entrepreneur finds a way to meet the demand with their supply. This entrepreneurship can be beneficial for countries as it provides an avenue for people to generate their income and sustain themselves. Therefore, for this study, entrepreneurship is referred to as the development of new business opportunities to make a profit. Likewise, an entrepreneur would be defined as the individual that engages in entrepreneurship.

Several countries grappling with unemployment have used entrepreneurship as a solution. The following subsections review the experience of selective countries, namely Nigeria, Malaysia, and Singapore.

2.1 Nigeria

In the 2000s in Nigeria, the Federal Government adopted small and medium-scale entrepreneurs (SMEs) as the building block of the country's economy. Unfortunately, the large volume of unemployed youth and able-bodied adults did not have the requisite skills for entrepreneurship. This prompted the Yaraduah administration to include entrepreneurship and wealth creation as the number three item of its Seven-Point Agenda. Education was identified as the vehicle to promote entrepreneurship, subsequently, the government directed the National Universities Commission (NUC) to commence with entrepreneurship education. This resulted in all tertiary education institutions in Nigeria including a compulsory entrepreneurship course as part of the curriculum for all programs from the 2007/2008 academic year (Nwekeaku 2013).

The policy direction of mandatory entrepreneurship training was needed in Nigeria, especially since the country's education system, which was inherited from its colonial era, was geared towards maintaining administrative control. Emphasis was placed on rote learning, and producing personnel with administrative skills, and teachers.[2] This was a contrast to the creativity and innovations, and the willingness to explore new business ventures, which are the key tenants behind the growth of many advanced economies (Nwekeaku 2013).

Nigeria's mandatory entrepreneurship training was met with several obstacles. First, the country's universities lack sufficient manpower for effective teaching and learning of entrepreneurship education in the country. As the available stock of teachers does not have the skills to cope with the

[2] Ironically, European countries have long abandoned their old education systems, and emphasis in the tertiary institutions is placed on developing more knowledge, and building the innovative and creative skills of students (Nwekeaku 2013).

challenges of the new curriculum. Since an individual cannot give what they do not possess, then lecturing by the existing stock of lecturers may not provide the desired results (Tope et al. 2014).

Second, the government's mandatory entrepreneurship training appeared as an adhoc directive without sufficient planning and preparation. Nwekeaku (2013) notes that a pilot study should have been implemented before making any national commitment.

Third, no special funding was made available to achieve the government's objective. Obeleagu-Nzelibe and Moruku (2010) note that Nigeria's universities are in urgent need of funding to train the lecturers, purchase infrastructure and make the necessary preparations to properly implement the mandatory entrepreneurship mandate.

2.2 Malaysia

In Malaysia's Malaysia Vision 2020 plan, the government indicated its goal of transforming the country into a knowledge-based economy by the year 2020. It envisioned that education would be a key tool in stimulating entrepreneurship and economic growth. Subsequently, the government made entrepreneurship subjects mandatory for all students at its country's public universities. It hoped that this policy directive would result in fewer unemployed graduates and an increase in business and entrepreneurship activity (Loh Rahim et al. 2015).

However, entrepreneurship education in Malaysia has earlier roots. In fact, in 1982, the Institut Teknologi MARA (ITM) introduced a compulsory co-curriculum called Kembara Usahawan (KEMUSA) which taught entrepreneurship education for students. Later in 1988, ITM introduced a mandatory subject called Fundamentals of Entrepreneurship (ETR300) for all diploma students.

Apart from the mandatory entrepreneurship education courses, the Government of Malaysia also launched several policies to encourage entrepreneurship. This is evidenced by:

i) The Malaysia Education Blueprint 2015–2025, aspired for the graduates to be equipped with the necessary leadership, knowledge, and thinking skills to thrive in business.
ii) The Entrepreneurship Action Plan 2016–2020, sought to 1) integrate elements of entrepreneurship across the curriculum, 2) create a job

creator framework, 3) improve the entrepreneurship ecosystem for graduates, and 4) strengthen the competencies of entrepreneurship lecturers (Nawawi et al. 2020).

Malaysian entrepreneurs have access to various financial instruments for their business endeavors, including business loans, venture capital, grants, and micro finance. In 2015, the Government of Malaysia passed legislation for the support of crowdfunding (Loh Rahim et al. 2015).

Despite the existence of the entrepreneurship education co-circumlum and the implementation of government policies, unemployment among university graduates persists. The Central Bank of Malaysia in March 2019 annual report notes that as of 2018, 173,457 diploma and degree holders penetrated Malaysia's job market, but only 98,514 high-skilled jobs were available (CBM 2019).

Several challenges hinder the greater adoption of entrepreneurship by university graduates in Malaysia. The main reasons include:

- Students continue to focus on grades rather than developing the acumen for business. Subsequently, many graduates are still reluctant to take risks and venture into business despite undergoing entrepreneurship training.
- The bureaucracy involved in obtaining loans is a deterrent to many graduates. Additionally, many graduates are not cognizant of all the financing options available, including microfinancing.
- Some lecturers were not given proper entrepreneurship training and lacked experience in business and entrepreneurship. Subsequently, they only teach business theories to the students but do not create the practical learning environment to help produce greater volumes of graduate entrepreneurs.

Nevertheless, the steps taken by the Government of Malaysia are creating an enabling environment for entrepreneurship, and may require more time to produce better results.

2.3 Singapore

Singapore, a small island city-state of approximately 728 km^2 in the Pacific, was under British colonial rule for over a century. After the British failed to protect Singapore from Japanese invasion during World War II, it led to strong anti-colonial sentiments within the country. Eventually, in 1963,

Singapore joined with Malaysia to secede from British rule. The subsequent state was called the Federation of Malaysia (Zhou 2019).

But the problems of Singapore did not end through the formation of the Federation of Malaysia. There was social conflict between the Singaporean and Malaysian populations. Eventually, the Malaysian parliament annexed Singapore from the Federation of Malaysia in 1965, resulting in Singapore's independence (Zhou 2019).

In the initial years after gaining independence, a large proportion of Singapore's labour force was unemployed. Furthermore, there was poor sanitation, a lack of proper public infrastructure, and inadequate water supply. Given that the country lacked mineral natural resources, the economic outlook appeared even more dismal (Blomqvist 2000; Zhou 2019). This prompted the Lee Kuan Yew administration to embark on a labour-intensive industrialization programme. Moreover, the Lee Kuan Yew administration networked with the developed world and convinced several multinational corporations to manufacture in Singapore (Zhou 2019).

To attract foreign investors, the government created an enabling environment that was safe, corruption-free, and charged low taxes. This was facilitated through the implementation of draconian[3], but business-friendly laws. Unsurprisingly, these policies were highly favoured by investors, and resulted in an influx of foreign direct investment (FDI) in Singapore, and prompted double-digit economic growth within the 1970s.

The policy direction of the Government of Singapore during the 1980s was focused on building human resource capacity to exploit new technologies (Nawaz and Koc 2020). The country also established several technical schools to train people in various technological and technical vocational areas. The co-curriculum of the educational institutes was periodically reviewed and updated to ensure that graduates are produced with the skills required for the targeted industries. Moreover, collaborations were developed with international corporations to facilitate the practical training of graduates in areas such as information, communication and technology (ICT), biotech research, pharmaceuticals, electrical engineering and electronics, and chemical engineering (Ng 2015; Zhou 2019). Graduates

[3] Some of the laws were draconian. For example, individuals that protested and threatened the authority of the government were quickly jailed without much due process. Nevertheless, these laws were effective in maintaining stability in the country.

that were unable to secure the high-end technology internships were enrolled in labour-intensive services such as tourism and transportation (Zhou 2019).

Singapore implemented several supporting initiatives to encourage research, innovation, and entrepreneurship. The support programmes include:

- Tax allowances and deductions
    - Reducing the corporate tax rate from 40% to 33% in 1986. Then to 17% in 2010.
    - In 1980, the government introduced the Research and Development Tax Allowance Scheme (RDTAS). This instituted a tax deduction for research.
    - The expansion of the RDAS in 1990 from only the manufacturing sector to include the services sector.
    - The revision of the RDAS in 2008 to form the Research and Development Tax Allowance Scheme (RDTAS) and Research and Development Incentive Scheme for Start-up Enterprise (RISE). The RDTAS and the RISE allowed a 100% tax deduction for all qualifying research expenditures inside of Singapore, and by citizens outside of Singapore.
    - In 2010, the government replaced RDTAS and RISE with the Productivity and Innovation Credit (PIC) programme which allowed for an additional 300% tax deduction on research up to 400,000 Singapore Dollar (SGD).
    - In 2014 the government introduced the "enhanced tax deduction for research and development" and the "super deduction for research and development". These additional allowances apply to projects that did not receive the PIC allowance. The projects must be approved by Singapore's Economic Development Board (EDB) and may receive 50% to 100% tax deduction.
- Technology transfer
    - In 1992, the National University of Singapore (NUS) launched the NUS Industry Liaison to facilitate technology transfer in Singapore.
- Research institutions
    - In 1991, the government formed the National Science and Technology Board (NSTB), and the Research and Development Assistance Scheme (RDAS). The organisation's objective was to facilitate collaborations among researchers inside and outside of Singapore.

  - In 2001, the NSTB was restructured as the Agency for Science, Technology and Research (ASTAR).
  - ASTAR and its two sub-divisions, namely the Biomedical Research Council (BMRC) and the Science and Engineering Research Council (SERC) provide oversight for research institutions in Singapore in the areas of biotechnology, medical technology, pharmacy, communications, chemicals, computational sciences, and manufacturing.
  - In 2006, the Campus for Research Excellence and Technological Enterprise (CREATE) was developed with the mandate of facilitating collaborations in research between institutions inside and outside of Singapore in the following areas: human systems, energy systems, environmental systems, and urban systems.
  - In 2007, the Research Centre of Excellence (RCE) was created to help strengthen research in the universities in Singapore in the following areas: earth science, quantum technology, cancer science, mechanobiology, and environmental life science.
  - In 2007, Centre of Innovation (COI) was operationalized with the mandate of encouraging partnerships between research institutions and industries, to produce research that will assist SMEs to upgrade their technological and innovative capacity.
- Science parks
  - In 1980, the government developed the first science park in Singapore.
  - In 1993, the government developed the second science park in Singapore.
- Innovation clusters
  - In 2003, the government created Biopolis, a biomedical research and technology cluster.
  - In 2008, the government created Fushionopolis, an ICT, physical sciences, and engineering cluster.
  - In 2020, the government launched Mediapolis, an ICT and media industry cluster. The innovation clusters also act as business incubators.
- Public-private partnerships
  - In 2002, the Nanyang Technological University (NTU) introduced its Technopreneurship and Innovation Program.

  - In 2009, the government commissioned the Research, Innovation, and Enterprise (RIE) to encourage public-private partnership programmes.[4]
- Intellectual property protection
  - There are laws in Singapore which protect intellectual property. They include the Patents Act, the Copyright Act, and the Trademark Act (Nawaz and Koc 2020).
- Immigration of labour
  - When Singapore became independent in 1965, it no longer allowed the free migration of people between Singapore and Malaysia. The migration policy shift as well as low fertility rates would have resulted in a significant decline in Singapore's labour force. Subsequently, Singapore allowed the entry of migrants, mainly from Canada, Europe, and the United States.
  - Migrant workers in Singapore are categorised into foreign talent and foreign workers. Foreign talent refers to university-qualified professionals. Foreign workers refer to foreign workers without a university degree.

This technological innovation model allowed Singapore to transition from an economy that was primarily engaged in the production and export of textiles, garments, and basic electronics in the 1970s to an economy participating in solar photovoltaic wafer production, logistics, biotech research, pharmaceuticals, integrated circuit design, and aerospace engineering in the 1990s (Zhou 2019; Nawaz and Koc 2020).

2.4 Summary Insight

A review of the experiences of Nigeria and Malaysia suggests that the education system can be adjusted to produce graduate entrepreneurs. However, entrepreneurship education programmes alone are not enough. The experience of Singapore reveals that a small developing country can develop an appropriate enabling environment for entrepreneurship by looking outwards for foreign capital and talent. However, government

---

[4] The projects implemented by RIE during its operation include: Technopreneurship21, Growing Enterprises with Technology Upgrade (Get-up), Corporate Laboratory Initiatives, National Innovation Challenge (NIC), Thematic R&D, Test Bedding and Demonstration of Innovation Research, ASTAR Collaborative Commerce Marketplace (ACCM), Collaborative Industry Projects (CIP), Partnerships for Capability Transformation (PACT), Technology Adoption Program (TAP), and Start-up/Gap Funds (Nawaz and Koc 2020).

policy would be key in triggering the technology and skills transfer. Additionally, due to the small size of the domestic market, entrepreneurs should consider developing goods and services for international markets from the start.

The next chapter reviews the labour market characteristics of the 3 selective hydrocarbon-rich CARICOM Member States. This assessment will provide insight into the labour market constraints faced by the respective countries.

CHAPTER THREE

CARICOM MEMBER STATES LABOUR MARKET OVERVIEW

The CARICOM Member States is a customs union in the Caribbean consisting mainly of English-speaking countries. It was established by the Treaty of Chaguaramas, which was initially signed by Barbados, Jamaica, Guyana, and T&T on 4 July 1973, but came into effect on August 1, 1973. This regional integration was the culmination of a 15-years of negotiation to fulfil the aspirations of regional solidarity which was born with the establishment of the British West Indies Federation in 1958 (Jones 2003).[5] The members are Antigua and Barbuda, Bahamas, Barbados, Belize, Dominica, Grenada, Guyana, Haiti, Jamaica, Montserrat, Saint Kitts and Nevis, Saint Lucia, Saint Vincent and the Grenadines, Suriname, and T&T.

The CARICOM Member States share their historical background as they were all former colonies of European countries. Their economies were structured to produce a few primary agricultural commodities for export to European markets. Additionally, except for Haiti and Suriname, the member

[5] The first attempt at regional integration in the Caribbean can be seen with the formation of the West Indian Federation among the English speaking Caribbean. This lasted over the 1958-1962 period. However, the desire for country sovereignty overpowered regional solidarity, and consequently the federation was short-lived. The second attempt at regionalism was the Caribbean Free Trade Association (CARIFTA) in 1965. As its name suggested, this was a free trade area formed between Caribbean islands and was geared towards increasing trade among the islands. CARIFTA was succeeded by the formation of CARICOM in 1973. Although its original aim was to be a common market, there were still restrictions to the movement of labour and the member states were not always uniform in the implementation of the common external tariff (CET). In 1989 CARICOM Heads of Government (HoG) decided to improve upon the implementation of a Caribbean common market. In 2006 CARICOM Single Market and Economy (CSME) was formed to build upon the CARICOM framework and effectively implement the Caribbean Common Market.

states are all English-speaking countries. Despite the historical background, language, and cultural similarities, the member states are heterogeneous.

One of the main notable differences of the Caribbean countries is size. The islands of Antigua and Barbuda, Barbados, Dominica, Grenada, Montserrat, St. Kitts and Nevis, St. Lucia, and St. Vincent and the Grenadines are small and occupy less than 751 km^2. The other member states are endowed with significantly larger land masses. Anguilla land area is only 91 km^2, in contrast to Jamaica whose land mass is 10,991 km^2. The Eastern Caribbean islands have a combined area of 2914 km^2 which represents 0.6% of CARICOM's land area. The islands' small size limits their ability to achieve economies of scale in production and ability to diversify into a wide range of activities (Romer 1986; and Barro and Sala-I-Martin 1995).

There is also a disparity in population size. Haiti has the largest population of 10.12 million (World Bank 2021). It is then followed by the populations of Jamaica and T&T which stand at 2.8 million and 1.3 million respectively. This is a big contrast to countries such as St. Kitts and Nevis, and Montserrat which have population sizes of 100,000 and 5,000 respectively. Haiti accounts for approximately 59% of CARICOM's population whereas Montserrat accounts for approximately 0.03%.

There are also differences in the size of GDP. T&T stood out with the largest real GDP of US$21.6 billion in 2020. This was followed by Jamaica with a GDP of US$13.8 billion, then the Bahamas with a GDP of US$9.9 billion. The smaller Islands such as Grenada, Dominica, St. Kitts and Nevis, Montserrat, and St. Vincent and the Grenadines also had the lowest GDP in the region. Table 3.1 summarises the economic performance of selective CARICOM Member States.

There are differences between the main revenue earning industries of the Caribbean countries. As previously mentioned, T&T is endowed with commercial reserves of hydrocarbons. This has allowed T&T to earn windfall revenue, especially over the 2000 to 2008 period while it experienced a boom in the export of liquefied natural gas (LNG) (Boopsingh and McGuire 2014). While at the time of writing, data was not publicly available, Guyana started to experience an uptick in its revenues from 2020 due to the export of crude oil. Suriname is also likely to experience a similar hydrocarbon boom when it starts the commercial export of crude oil.

Table 3.1: GDP, Population and Land Area of the CARICOM Member States

	Current GDP (2020)	pop mil	land size km^2
Antigua and Barbuda	$1,370,281,481	0.1	442
the Bahamas	$9,907,500,000	0.4	13,864
Barbados	$4,418,000,000	0.3	431
Belize	$1,636,280,797	0.3	22,966
Dominica	$504,214,815	0.1	750
Haiti	N.A.	10.12	27,750
Grenada	$1,042,100,556	0.1	345
Guyana	$5,471,256,595	0.8	214,970
Jamaica	$13,812,425,037	2.8	10,991
Montserrat	N.A.	0.005	103
St. Kitts and Nevis	$980,740,741	0.1	269
St. Lucia	$1,616,772,741	0.2	616
St. Vincent and the Grenadines	$807,474,074	0.1	389
Suriname	$2,884,248,048	0.5	163,820
T&T	$21,588,037,505	1.3	5,128

Source: World Bank (2021)

Apart from hydrocarbons, some member states also possess commodity natural resources. Guyana's economy is dominated by agriculture and extractive industries. The economy is based largely on the export of sugar, gold, bauxite, diamond, shrimp, lumber, and rice. Suriname's economy is heavily dependent upon the mining industry. Its main exports are alumina, gold, and oil, however, bananas, timber, agriculture, and fisheries are also significant sectors (Bermúdez-Lugo 2002). Jamaica is also rich with mineral natural resources as it mines and exports bauxite.

The other member states lack any mineral natural resources. Subsequently, they rely upon the export of primary agriculture commodities, as well as the tourism industry for the earning of export revenue (Downes 1998). Subsequently, the CARICOM Member States can be grouped into categories based on their export structure. The first is the goods-producing and exporting countries, namely Jamaica, Guyana, Suriname, and T&T. The second is the service-producing and exporting countries, namely Antigua and Barbuda, the Bahamas, Barbados, Dominica, Haiti, Grenada, Montserrat, St. Kitts and Nevis, St. Lucia, and St. Vincent and the Grenadines.

The next subsections review the labour market characteristics of the hydrocarbon-rich CARICOM Member States.

3.1 Labour Statistics of T&T

The size of the non-institutional population[6] in T&T was 991.1 thousand in 2009. Over the next 10 years, the non-institutional population grew to just over 1 million people. The labour force, which is the part of the non-institutional population that has work or is looking for work, managed to grow from 620.9 thousand to 634 thousand over the corresponding period. Since the growth in the labour force was smaller than the growth in the size of the non-institutional population, the labour force participation rate declined from 62.9% in 2009 to 59.1% in 2018. Table 3.02 provides an overview.

The proportion of people categorised as "not part of the labour force" grew to 40.9% in 2018 from 37.4% in 2009. Since these people are not institutionalised, they are typically excluded from the estimation of the labour force as they are regarded as discouraged workers.

There were 32.6 thousand people unemployed in T&T in 2009. This number contracted to 24.9 thousand in 2018. Subsequently, the unemployment rate contracted from 5.3% to 3.9% over the 10-year period. Since full employment unemployment is typically around 5%, it suggests that the economy of T&T may be around full employment.

The consideration of the unemployed proportion of the labour force is an under-representation of the number of people without jobs. Since the labour force participation rate in 2018 was 59.1%, it meant that 40.9% of the non-institutional population had no job. This share was approximately 438.6 thousand people. When the number of discouraged workers is added to the unemployed people, it reveals that the total number of people without jobs was 438.6 thousand in 2018.

The labour force can be decomposed based on gender. Females tend to comprise approximately 40% of the labour force in T&T (World Bank 2021).

---

[6] The non-institutional population refers to the part of the population that are not in any institution. In other words, it refers to the people in the population that are not in schools, hospitals, jails, and other institutions.

Table 3.02: Labour Market Statistics for T&T (2009-2018)

	Persons with Jobs (000's)	Labour Force (000's)	Unemployment (000's)	Unemployment Rate (%)	Non-Institutional Population (000's)	Participation Ratio (%)
2018	609.1	634.0	24.9	3.9	1072.4	59.1
2017	603.3	633.9	30.6	4.8	1071.3	59.2
2016	613	638.3	25.2	3.9	1068.5	59.7
2015	623.3	645.3	22.0	3.4	1065.1	60.6
2014	636.8	658.6	21.8	3.3	1063.4	61.9
2013	626.3	650.1	23.9	3.7	1059.6	61.4
2012	614.1	646.0	31.9	4.9	1044.1	61.9
2011	585.3	616.4	31.1	5.1	1005.7	61.3
2010	582.2	618.9	36.7	5.9	997.0	62.1
2009	588.3	620.9	32.6	5.3	991.1	62.6

Source: CBTT (2022)

Youth unemployment is also an important characteristic of the labour market. The youth labour force, the people in the 15 to 24 years' age category that are not institutionalised and are willing to work, tend to have a higher unemployment rate than the overall labour force.

In 2011, approximately 35% of the total unemployed in T&T were young persons. The youth unemployment rate was recorded at 12.1%. The female youth unemployment rate was 16.4%, while the youth unemployment rate for males was 9.3% (PRTT 2012). The GORTT MSDFS (2017) notes that the youth unemployment rate rose from 8.1% to 11.6% over the 2013 to 2016 period. The GORTT MSDFS (2017) blamed the economic contraction in T&T experienced over the 2014 to 2016 period, in lieu of weak energy prices, for the rise in youth unemployment over the corresponding period.

3.2 Labour Statistics of Guyana

Guyana's population in 2020 stood at 786,559 people (World Bank 2021). The country's labour force was 280,850 people in 2012 and grew to 308,188 people by 2017. The labour force is mainly composed of men. This is evidenced by 68.3% of the labour force being male in 2012, and 60.1% (191,921 people) being male in 2017. However, the participation of women in the labour force in Guyana has increased in both absolute terms and relative terms from 31.67% (88,929 people) in 2012 to 39.92% (123,025 people) in 2017. See Table 3.03.

The unemployment rate in Guyana was 12.5% in 2012 and remained relatively unchanged at 12% by 2017. Given that the labour force participation rate was 56% in 2017, it suggested that the working-age population was 550,336 people.[7] Therefore, 444% of the working-age population, which equates to approximately 242,148 people were out of work in Guyana in 2017. Given that the total number of unemployed people in Guyana in 2017 was 37,119, it suggested that approximately 205,028 people were categorised as discouraged workers.

The youth unemployment rate was also high in Guyana. It stood at 21.6% in 2017.

[7] 308,188 * 100/56 = 550,336 people.

Table 3.03: Population & Labour Force (Guyana)

Population aged 15+ (thousand persons)	2012 (from Census)	2017, Third Quarter	
	Total persons	Total persons	% of total working age population
Men	247,583	268,864	48.8
Women	256,742	281,966	51.2
Total	504,325	550,831	100
Labour force (thousand persons)	Persons	Persons	As percentage of total labour force
Men	191,921	185,163	60.1
Women	88,929	123,025	39.9
Total	280,850	308,188	100
Labour force participation rate (%)	2012	2017, Third Quarter	
Men	77.5	68.9	
Women	34.6	43.6	
Total	55.7	56.0	

Source: IDB, BSG, ILO (2017)

Table 3.04: Unemployment in Guyana

	2012	2017, Third Quarter	
Unemployed population (thousand)		Persons	As % of total unemployed
Men	20,172	18,290	49.3
Women	14,792	18,829	50.7
Total	34,964	37,119	100
Unemployment rate (%)	2012	2017, Third Quarter	
Men	10.6	9.9	
Women	16.7	15.3	
Total	12.5	12.0	

Employed population	2012	2017, Third Quarter Total persons	% of total employed population
Men	170,905	166,873	61.6
Women	73,930	104,195	38.4
Total	244,835	271,068	100.00
Employment to population ratio (%)	2012	2017, Third Quarter	
Men	66.3	62.1	
Women	28.0	36.9	
Total		49.2	
Unemployed youth (thousand persons)	2012	Persons	Youth unemployment rate (%) (2017)
Men	10176	7,873	17.3
Women	6635	8,588	28.0
Total		16,462	21.6

Source: IDB, BSG, ILO (2017)

3.3 Labour Statistics of Suriname

The unemployment rate in Suriname was 8.10% in 2012, and marginally decreased to 6.942% by 2019. However, given a labour force participation rate of 56.62% in 2012, it suggested that there were 460,862 non-institutionalised able-bodied people without work. If this is added to the 16,194 unemployed people in 2012, the total number of people without work would increase to 47,7056 people. Similarly, given a labour force participation rate of 56.83% in 2019, the number of "discouraged workers" would be 386,252 people. When this is added to the 15,234 unemployed people in 2019, the total number of people without work would rise to 40,1486 people.

Youth unemployment is also high in Suriname. The youth unemployment rate was 20.59% in 2012, but it declined to 13.32% in 2019, largely on the account of more youth being categorised as "discouraged workers".

Females account for approximately 38% of the labour force in Suriname (World Bank 2021).

Table 3.05: Labour Statistics in Surname

	2012	2017	2019
labour force	199,922	214,449	219,507
working age population	353,094	377,153	386,252
labour force participation rate	56.62	56.86	56.83%
unemployment rate	8.10%	7.80%	6.94%
youth unemployment rate	20.59%	13.31%	13.32%

Source: World Bank (2021)

3.4 Shifting Employment

The agricultural sector was historically the main absorber of labour in Guyana, Suriname, and T&T. In 1970, the earliest year with available data, the agricultural sector accounted for 23% of the employed labour force in T&T (Downes 1998). For Guyana, the agriculture share of employment was 32.45% in 1991 (World Bank 2021). For Suriname, the agriculture share of employment was 56% in 1954 (Mhango 1991). This high employment share in the Caribbean region was a result of the countries' preferential access to the European market under the Lomé agreements.[8]

In 1993, European countries deepened their integration and formally established the European Union (EU) as an economic and political union. The Single European Market (SEM)[9] was a component of the economic union, and it required all member countries to reform their import policy. At the inception of the EU, the preferential import regime was extended to exporters from the African Caribbean and Pacific (ACP) countries. However, with the conclusion of the Uruguay Round of the General Agreement on Tariffs and Trade (GATT), and the formation of the World Trade Organisation (WTO) in 1995, there was an increased push to enforce

[8] The first Lomé Convention (Lomé I) was signed in 1975. Lomé II was signed on 31 October 1979 and covered the 1980 to 1985 period. Lomé III was signed on 8 December 1984 and covered the 1985 to 1990 period. Lomé IV was signed on 15 December 1989 and covered the 1990 to 2000 period (ACP Secretariat 2003).

[9] The SEM allowed the free movement of goods between the EU member states. The SEM also ended the 12 separate systems under which individual European countries could import agricultural products from the African Caribbean and Pacific (ACP) countries under the Lomé IV (Klak et al. 2011).

non-discrimination in trade rules.[10] In 1995, the United States (US) government, acting on behalf of the multinational corporations which had banana interests in Central and South America, packaged a coalition composed of Guatemala, Honduras, and Mexico, and later Ecuador to raise a dispute at the WTO (Patterson 2001; COHA 2005). The plaintiffs argued that the EU's agricultural import regime under Lomé IV was discriminatory, and not consistent with the WTO's rules on non-discrimination. In 1996, the WTO Dispute Settlement Body ruled in favour of the plaintiffs. After several appeals, the WTO Dispute Settlement Body ruled that the EU-ACP banana regime was not fully compatible with WTO regulations (COHA 2005).

These developments caused a change in the EU import regime. The EU had to gradually reduce the trade preferences offered to the ACP to be compliant with the WTO rules. More importantly, the EU eventually dismantled the Sugar Protocol, which paid prices higher than the world price of sugar. The loss of these trade preferences caused the sugar industry in Guyana, Suriname, and T&T to become less profitable.

Recognising these international changes, as well as the productivity challenges experienced domestically, in 2003 the GORTT decided to close down its national sugar company, Caroni 1975 Limited, which was incurring loss (Allard 2012; Charles 2019).[11] The closure of Caroni 1975 Limited directly resulted in the retrenchment of 9,200 workers. As a long-

[10] The first article of the General Agreement on Tariffs and Trade (GATT), which governs trade in goods, requires unconditional and universal most-favored-nation (MFN) treatment among all members. The principle of national treatment, requires that the products of locals and foreigners should be treated equally (VanGrasstek 2013). If these 2 principles were applied to ACP countries trading with the EU under the Lomé agreements, then the ACP countries should have been engaging in reciprocated trade. Since the ACP countries are non-member countries of the EU, they should have been facing the same MFN tariff imposed on all non-EU member countries. Otherwise, the principle of national treatment would require that all non-EU member countries receive the same preferential access to the EU market, which the ACP countries were receiving.

[11] Caroni 1975 Limited incurred annual operating losses of TT$175 million in 1996, TT$246 million in 1997, TT$305 million in 1998, TT$223 million in 1999, TT$349 million in 2000, and TT$367 million in 2001. The GORTT subvention allocation to Caroni 1975 Limited was TT$346 million in 1996, TT$124 million in 1997, TT$190 million in 1998, TT$808 million in 1999, TT$388 million in 2000, TT$188 million in 2001, and TT$579 million in 2002 (Shah 2016).

term implication, the agriculture share of employment in T&T declined to approximately 3% of the labour force by 2018 (CBTT 2022).

T&T was fortunate to already be earning hydrocarbon revenues when the erosion of trade preferences was occurring in the 1990s. Subsequently, the government was able to absorb a large share of the labour force in the public service and state-owned organisations. The dependence on the hydrocarbon sector results in T&T's economy being "dual-structured". The energy sector has also been described as an 'enclave' (Boopsingh 2004). The energy sector earns the bulk of the revenue, but it generates very little direct employment. Consequently, the government acts as the medium to connect the energy sector to the rest of the economy, through taxation and transfers. Hence the reason why the government share of employment was able to increase to approximately 60% of the labour force by 2018 (CBTT 2022).

In Guyana, the erosion of preferences also caused a decline in agriculture share of employment. By 2019, the agriculture share of employment was only 15.44% (World Bank 2021). Unfortunately, Guyana's hydrocarbon boom did not start in the 1990s, so the government was not able to operate "make work" programmes. Therefore, the farmers negatively affected by the erosion of trade preferences responded by seeking work in other primary commodity extractive industries, such as gold mining, bauxite extraction, fishing, and lumber extraction. The people that were unable to find work either emigrated, became unemployed, or were classified as "discouraged workers".

Similarly, the agriculture share of employment declined to 8.08% in Surname by 2019 (World Bank 2021), on account of the decline in trade preferences. The farmers responded by finding work in other primary commodity extractive industries including the bauxite, gold, and lubber industries. The youths that were unable to obtain work in the extractive industries either emigrated, became unemployed, or were classified as "discouraged workers".

3.5 Summary Insight

The CARICOM Member States have a similar colonial history, but are heterogeneous with regards to land size, population size, and economic activity. Differences also exist between the hydrocarbon-rich CARICOM Member States. Presently, T&T has the highest GDP, and can keep its unemployment rate suppressed at below the 5% full employment-unemployment rate.

Guyana and Suriname also are richly endowed with commercial hydrocarbon reserves, but they are entering the hydrocarbon trade industry almost a century after T&T. Given the erosion to trade preferences that occurred in the 1990s, as well as the limited opportunities in the associated period, the most recent statistics for Guyana, and Suriname reflect double-digit unemployment rates.

The unemployment rate does not give a full insight into why people in a country remain without work. The next chapter dives deeper into the unemployment situation to help generate an understanding of the problem.

CHAPTER FOUR

UNDERSTANDING UNEMPLOYMENT AND UNDEREMPLOYMENT

Despite the abundance of hydrocarbon natural resources, many people are without work in the hydrocarbon-rich CARICOM Member States. Downes (1998) proposes 4 reasons for the high unemployment rate in T&T. These reasons include: i) the relatively high capital intensity of the energy sector;[12] ii) the stickiness of wages at levels higher than labour productivity; iii) the lack of information on vacancies;[13] and iv) the inadequacy of the education and training system.[14] The reasons proposed by Downes (1998) were valid in the 1990s, however, the economic circumstances of the citizens of T&T have changed significantly in the past 2 decades.

Gafar (2004) notes that unemployment has traditionally been high in Guyana, due to the lingering effects of the erosion of trade preferences, as well as structural problems in Guyana's economy. Additionally, youth unemployment has also been high in Guyana due to their inexperience.

Vos et al. (1999) highlight that unemployment in Suriname has closely been associated with the performance of its economy.

---

[12] T&T's economy is often referred to as being "dual sectored". The energy sector earns the bulk of the revenue, but as it is capital intensive it hires a small percentage of the labour force. Subsequently, the government acts as the medium to connect the energy sector to the rest of the economy. It charges taxes on the energy sector, which generates funds to finance expenditure on various transfers and subsidies.

[13] In the 2010s, there is high accessibility to the internet in T&T. Once an employer advertises a job online, people will see the advertised vacancy.

[14] With the introduction of GATE, citizens in T&T are able to pursue training in any area of their choice. Therefore, this reason proposed by Downes (1998) is no longer valid.

Based on several interviews with stakeholders in 2019,[15] the main reasons that have been identified for the unemployment problem in the hydrocarbon-rich CARICOM Member States are: i) macroeconomic shocks and structural economy-wide problems; ii) the lack of experience of young workers; iii) the excess supply of skilled labour; iv) inefficiency in hiring by the main employers; v) inefficiency in the government's on-the–job training programme. The following sections examine these problems in greater detail.

4.1 Macroeconomic Shocks and Economy-Wide Problems

T&T, Guyana, and Suriname have all experienced macroeconomic shocks which negatively impacted their respective economies and employment rate.

For instance, T&T earned windfall oil revenues in the 1970s due to the Organisation of Petroleum Exporting Countries (OPEC) oil embargoes and high oil prices of 1973 and 1979. The government's coffers filled, the real GDP grew by 6% per annum over the 1974 to 1981 period, and by 1980, the country's total foreign currency reserves had grown to an equivalent to 14 months of import cover (Weissman 1990).

In 1983 oil prices crashed, and T&T was immediately faced with a balance of trade deficit. The GORTT, unable to finance this deficit, sought financing from international markets, but found weak success despite its good credit track record. Unable to attract adequate financing to cover its balance of payments deficit, the GORTT adopted austerity measures. In December 1985, the government devalued it's the exchange rate from 1 USD = 2.40 USD to 1 USD = 3.6 TTD (Weissman 1990). There was a change in political administration in 1986,[16] followed by the implementation of more austerity measures in 1987. The measures included the suspension of the cost of living allowance (COLA) for public servants, reduction of government

[15] The author held discussions with stakeholders in the CARICOM Member States while employed with the Economic Commission for Latin America and the Caribbean (ECLAC) in 2019.

[16] On December 15, 1986, the National Alliance for Reconstruction (NAR) defeated the People's National Movement (PNM) in T&T's general election.

expenditure on transfers and subsidies, and the privatisation of some state-owned enterprises[17] (Downes 1998).

Facing liquidity and solvency constraints, the GORTT sought financial support from the International Monetary Fund (IMF) in 1988. As a condition of the loan, the GORTT implemented several measures, including the devaluation of the exchange rate to 1 USD = 4.24 TTD, salary freezes, a 10% cut in public sector wages, further reductions in subsidies, the introduction of a value-added tax (VAT), the removal of items on the import negative list, increases in tariffs, limits on accumulated external debt, increases in the discount rate, the removal of all remaining price controls, and limits on the Central Banks loans to commercial banks (Downes 1998). Collectively, these measures reduced the economic activity in T&T, and caused a decline in employment from the 1980s onwards to the 1990s.

In Guyana, after the country gained its independence from colonial rule, the newly elected government pursued socialist and nationalisation strategies for development. This resulted in the government funding education from preschool to tertiary level for all Guyanese citizens in the 1970s (Danns 1992). The government also nationalised key sectors, including bauxite, sugar, and some financial institutions. By 1988, the government accounted for 85% of the investment in the country. Unfortunately, the government's administration and governance of the state-owned organisations were characterised by bureaucracy, and inefficiency. Eventually, that state-owned organisation became loss-making institutions that were a burden on Guyana's national treasury. Furthermore, the government also faced rising public debt, high inflation, declining foreign exchange reserves, fiscal and balance of trade deficits which led to its bankruptcy (Gafar 2004).

Over the 1978 to 1988 period, the GoG experimented with several policies aimed at arresting the economic contraction in Guyana. The adopted measures included the offering of incentives to exporters, introducing exchange rate controls, relaxing exchange rate controls, introducing trade restrictions, relaxing trade restrictions, and monetary policy adjustments. These policies were ineffective in turning around Guyana's economy as they were inconsistent and didn't consider the holistic impact on the economy (Danns 1998). Subsequently, in 1988, the government turned to the IMF for assistance (Danns 1998; Gafar 2004).

---

[17] At the time many of T&T's state-owned institutions were highly inefficient, and siphoning financial resources (Weissman 1990).

As a requirement of IMF loans, the GoG was mandated to implement a structural adjustment programme, which required several caveats, including the privatisation of state-owned enterprises, the reduction in subsidies, the reduction in government spending, a commitment to balance the budget, removal of price controls, increased fees for public services, and the depreciation of the exchange rate. These policies reduced both aggregate expenditure and aggregate demand in Guyana's economy (Gafar 2004). Moreover, the economic decline, as well as the erosion of trade preferences in the 1990s contributed to the high unemployment in Guyana from the 1980s to the 2010s.

Suriname, like its CARICOM neighbours, was historically a plantation colony. Bauxite production and export gained prominence in Suriname since World War II, and remained the major export commodity even after the country gained independence in 1975. The mining and export of gold also brought in significant revenues to the country. Additionally, the extraction of oil by the state-owned enterprise, Staatsolie, commenced in 1982 (van Dijck et al. 2000).

Bauxite, gold, and oil are primary commodities, and are subject to price volatility. Moreover, unexpected increases in the price of primary commodities have the potential to trigger inflationary effects, the appreciation of the real exchange rate, and the corresponding Dutch Disease effects if the windfall revenues are not adequately sterilised. The Dutch Disease problem becomes more apparent at the end of the primary commodity boom, and other sectors are considered for their revenue earning potential, but they cannot perform as they have become deindustrialized.

While Suriname was vulnerable to volatility in the primary commodity prices, a large part of its economic difficulty can be attributed to the country's political instability. After the military coup in 1980, there was a suspension of foreign aid, the stagnation of private foreign investment, leading to the decline of the mineral exports. Raids by a guerrilla group disrupted bauxite production, and caused economic stagnation. Although a general election was held in 1987, the political stability remained fragile. Another coup occurred in 1990, but political pressure from the US, and the Netherlands forced the militants to allow a general election in 1991. Despite the return to democracy, Suriname faced several seemingly intractable problems, including the proliferation of drug trafficking, gold smuggling, and widening social and economic inequalities (Ramsoedh 2016). These social-economic problems are mainly responsible for the unemployment in Suriname.

4.2 Lack of Experience of Young Workers and the Flawed Education System

Work experience is often cited as the main reason why some employers refuse to hire young people (González-Velosa et al. 2016). In some jobs, especially technical jobs, this reason is valid since technical knowledge is required to effectively perform these jobs.

In the CARICOM Member States, primary and secondary school education is free and mandatory for all citizens. Children tend to enter the primary school system between 3 to 5 years, and then they may proceed on to secondary school upon passing the national secondary school entrance examination. The average student may spend at least 7 years in primary school, and 5 years in secondary school before entering the labour market. After the completion of secondary school at the Form 5 level, some students may spend 2 years pursuing A-levels, while others may pursue technical vocational training. The students that go on to pursue tertiary education may spend an additional 3 years at a university. Therefore, by the time a person reaches the age of 18 or 19, they could have spent 15 years in school. If that person pursued tertiary education, by the time they have reached the age of 21 or 22 years, they could have spent at least 18 years in school. If after 15 to 18 years of school, a person does not have the required skills to allow them to work, it reflects a fundamental flaw in the educational system.

Several authors have recognised that the education system in the CARICOM Member States is flawed. One author asserts

> *"The education and training system has inadequately prepared the youth for the world of work"* (Downes 1998, 17).

Another author asserts

> *"The Trinidad and Tobago model is largely derived from the British colonial system. Regardless of its merits at that time, the instructional method is fundamentally out of touch with modern realities"* (Foss 2013, 92).

Foss (2013) goes on to criticise the teaching method, as well as the curriculum content in T&T's educational system.

> *"From a pedagogical perspective, the rote learning "talk and chalk" approach that treats all pupils equally regardless of ability is an anachronism being updated globally to include differentiated, participatory, and critical thinking methodologies. The content and focus of instruction is similarly outdated, with schools prioritising academic successes over that of*

> *life skills, technical/vocational skills, and basic literacy and numeracy"* (Foss 2013, 92).

Wolff (2009) notes that Guyana technical-vocational institutions all operate on outdated models of training, with inadequate curriculum, and poor or nonexistent collaboration with industry. The author indicates that this deficiency is common across the Caribbean.

> "*Most Caribbean institutions are not adequately responsive to labor requirements, and most do not tie their programs of study to labor market needs. Only a very few institutions actively trace their graduates to rate the success of their training. Structural unemployment, especially of young people, will complicate these assessments, but, in any event, more attention needs to be paid to tracking graduates. In most cases, curriculum is still based on academic criteria rather than being "competency-based," starting with occupational analysis*" (Wolff 2009, 183).

Jules (2008) remarked

> "*As each Caribbean country attained independence, access to education became a primary political imperative. For the masses, it meant opportunity for personal advancement, better jobs and a way out of poverty. For the ruling elites, the extension of basic provision signaled their modernising intent... To assuage the democratic aspirations for 'equity' of access in that period, meritocratic devices, such as scholarship schemes which facilitated access to secondary and tertiary education on a highly competitive basis, were established.*
>
> *Given this historical context, it can be said that Anglophone Caribbean education systems evolved maintaining the general architecture of the systems prevailing in the metropole. It is a historical fact that only in those countries and in those periods characterised by radical nationalist regimes was there any departure from the postcolonial paradigm and any attempt at rethinking of education. The bold measures taken in Cuba for the reform of education in the early revolutionary period involving the radical widening of access to education and the articulation of a cradle to grave educational paradigm established that a new and different conception of education in the Caribbean was possible. The Cheddi Jagan regime in Guyana (late 1950s) made education a cornerstone of national development establishing the University of Guyana in 1963; influenced by the Cuban successes*" (Jules 2008, 205).

Apart from the shortcomings identified by the previous authors, the recent COVID-19 pandemic has introduced new challenges to the education system. Country-wide lockdowns that were implemented by many countries were accompanied by many school children losing access to face-to-face education.

Alicia Bárcena, Executive Secretary of ECLAC, stressed

> "*The COVID-19 pandemic opens an opportunity to rethink and restructure education systems in Latin America and the Caribbean, and tackle the profound "silent crisis" that this sector is going through so as to prevent a generational catastrophe*" (cited in ECLAC 2021, 1).

Indeed, there is a consensus that the CARICOM Member States' present education system does not properly prepare young people for the world of work. The emphasis is on exams and route learning rather than the holistic development of the youth. Furthermore, there is a very weak connection between the academic environment and the industry.

Given that COVID-19 pandemic forced many academic institutions to rethink the means of delivery through the offering of virtual classes, it is certainly an appropriate time for policy makers in the CARICOM Member States to restructure the entire education system. The education system should be designed to suit the needs of the respective countries, and prepare the youth for the employment opportunities that are available after graduation. Moreover, the focus should also be placed on developing more graduate entrepreneurs rather than job-seeking graduates.

4.3 Excess Supply of Skilled Labour

One of the more common reasons proposed for the persistence of unemployment is the prevalence of structural unemployment (Downes 1998). One author notes

> *"much of the 'open' unemployment observed in Trinidad and Tobago is due to structural factors such as the nature of the educational system and its interface with the labor market (i.e., the mismatch problem), technological change, permanent shifts in the demand for goods and services and the skill content of the labor force"* (Downes 1998, 15).

While this reason may have been accurate in explaining the unemployment in the 1990s, the labour market dynamics changed in T&T in the 2000s.

As mentioned in Chapter One, in 2004, the GORTT introduced the GATE programme. Over the 2004 to 2015 period, the GORTT spent over TT$ 5 billion funding the GATE programme. Table 4.01 displays the funding information for GATE.

Table 4.01 GORTT Expenditure on GATE

Fiscal Year	No. Students Funded	Government Annual Expenditure
2004/2005	19,154	$102,193,273.00
2005/2006	29,170	$179,689,121.00
2006/2007	55,703	$472,771,454.00
2007/2008	53,857	$501,783,052.00
2008/2009	55,808	$574,435,788.72
2009/2010	53,483	$584,699,644.92
2010/2011	50,919	$611,646,565.05
2011/2012	59,455	$757,641,659.87
2012/2013	55,733	$720,775,071.50
2013/2014	49,406	$632,759,633.93
2014/2015	47,231	$699,884,393.33
Total	529,919	$5,838,279,657.32

Source: Simms et al. (2016)

Over 500 thousand citizens of T&T benefited from the GATE programme over the 2004 to 2015 period. As the GATE programme offered funding to all tertiary education areas, and not at targeted disciplines, people pursued education in any area of their choice.

Although multiple universities are operating in T&T, they generally offer degree programmes in at least one of the following areas: i) social science; ii) humanities; iii) law; iv) natural science; v) engineering; and vi) medicine.[18] Therefore, the GATE programme has facilitated an increased supply of various technical labour in T&T, effectively eliminating structural unemployment.

In contrast, the employment opportunities in T&T tend to be limited to a few skills. Table 4.02 provides an overview.

---

[18] It is noteworthy that the exact name that the different universities call their faculty may differ. However, the universities tend to offer degree programmes in the aforementioned areas.

Table 4.02: Types of Skills Required in Various Sectors

Sector	Skills required
Public service (government ministries and agencies)[19]	administration,[20] project management, policy,[21] accounting, legal, security, general maintenance
State-owned agencies	technical vocational,[22] administration, project management, accounting, legal, security, general maintenance
Teaching	all disciplines
Finance and banking	finance, accounting, administration, legal, security, general maintenance
Energy sector[23]	engineering, technical vocational, navigation and maritime studies, project management, legal, accounting, administration, food preparation, safety, security, general maintenance
Entertainment sector	media skills,[24] singing and dancing, cosmetics,[25] craft, event management, legal, accounting, project management, technical vocational, general maintenance, security, food preparation
Hotel and accommodation	administration, legal, accounting, technical vocational, general maintenance, security, food preparation

[19] It is notable that United Nations (UN) agencies tend to provide technical support to government ministries and agencies in T&T. Therefore, they tap into the same pool of skilled workers as the government ministries and agencies.

[20] Administration includes services such as human resource administration, marketing, and clerical duties.

[21] Policy includes economic, social, and environmental policy.

[22] Technical vocational includes services such as mechanical maintenance, electrical maintenance, wood working, instrumentation, computer networking and information technology, production operations, welding and metal work, surveying, masonry, etc.

[23] The energy sector includes oil, natural gas, downstream industries, and the companies supplying support services.

[24] Media skills include photography, videography, photo and video editing, graphic design, and music playing (disk jockey).

[25] Cosmetics include skills such as hair design, nail design, and the application of make-up.

Agro-processing	technical vocational, administration, project management, accounting, legal, security, general maintenance
Private sector stores[26]	administration, legal, accounting, general maintenance, security, food preparation
Health	medical, administration, legal, accounting, general maintenance, security, food preparation
Construction	technical vocational, project management, accounting, legal, security, general maintenance
Agriculture	open to anyone
Self-employed business[27]	open to anyone

As can be seen in Table 4.02, the most common (mode) employment opportunities are in administration, technical vocational, general maintenance, and security. Other common employment opportunities are in legal, accounting, project management, and food preparation. This limited range of employment opportunities has significant implications for graduates of the GATE-funded programmes.

Graduates that complete highly specialised programmes in social science, humanities, and natural science may find difficulty in obtaining employment in their field. For example, graduates that completed a BSc in Meteorology, or an MSc in Biomedical Physics may find difficulty in obtaining Meteorology or Biomedical Physics jobs.

While engineering skills are highly desirable in the energy sector in T&T, there is weak demand for these skills outside of the energy sector. For example, graduates that completed their BSc in Petroleum Engineering, would not find a Petroleum Engineering job in T&T outside of the energy sector. Furthermore, while these skills are highly valuable to specific employers, these skills may not be useful to other employers. For example, a graduate with a BSc in Petroleum Engineering, or BSc in Hydrology cannot sell petroleum engineering and hydrology services to the average

[26] Private sector stores include supermarkets, fast food chains, restaurants, stores in malls, and small and medium businesses owned by private individuals.

[27] Self-employed businesses include small business operations such as taxi services, the sale of food and beverages, the sale of clothes, the sale of imported goods, and the offering of technical vocational services on a project basis.

person. Therefore, graduates of these highly specialised degrees most likely will need to rely upon an employer to obtain a job. Additionally, graduates of highly specialised degrees that do not find employment in their field of study may find themselves competing with graduates of more generalised degrees for the available jobs.

By the end of 2021, Guyana and Suriname did not have an excess supply of skilled labour problem. There was presently a shortage of specialised skilled labour for the hydrocarbon industry in Guyana. This is largely due to the country being in the early stage of its hydrocarbon industry's life cycle. With a population size of approximately 800 thousand people and proven oil reserves of over 8 billion barrels, an excess supply of skilled labour is unlikely to develop in Guyana within the next decade. Nevertheless, it would augur well for Guyana and Suriname to avoid this problem by focusing on developing graduate entrepreneurs. This idea is discussed in greater detail in Chapter Six.

4.4 Inefficiency in Public Sector Hiring

4.4.1 Permanent Employment in the Public Service

In the Colonial Era before Independence, the colonies used service commissions to advise the Governor on the selection and appointment of candidates and to work in the public service. Upon independence, the former colonies retained their service commissions.

T&T, Guyana, and Suriname each possess: i) a Judicial and Legal Service Commission; ii) a Police Service Commission; iii) a Public Service Commission; and iv) a Teaching Service Commission.

The service commissions have the authority to:

- appoint persons to hold or act in the office of Commissioner and Deputy Commissioner;
- make appointments on promotion, transfer, and the confirmation of appointments of public servants;
- to remove and exercise disciplinary action over persons holding or acting in the aforementioned offices; and
- to enforce standards of conduct on such officers.

The service commissions are written in the constitution, thus making their structure difficult to change without constitutional reform and a special majority vote in Parliament.

The service commission system is very slow. It can take several years for a person that applies for a position to be contacted by the corresponding service commission to assume employment duties in that position. Additionally, the application system is paper-based rather than computerised, therefore documents in an applicant's file can go 'missing' during the application process.

Due to the tardiness in hiring, as well as the retiring of several workers in batches, there are thousands of vacancies in the public service of the respective countries.[28] Additionally, there is also inefficiency in prompting people in the public service. Although promotion should be based on the combination of qualification, knowledge, and competence, in practice, promotion in the public service is often based on seniority, and the length of employment.

The GORTT has long recognised that its public service operations are inefficient. Subsequently, it has commissioned several initiatives since 1964 to reform the public service. Table 4.03 provides a summary.

The GoG also acknowledged the structural deficiencies in its public service and has attempted public service reform. In 1991, the Desmond Hoyte-led administration introduced a series of reforms including the reduction in the number of ministries from 18 to 11, and restructured ministries by eradicating duplicate and overlapping tasks among government departments. These measures, although they were beneficial, were inadequate to address the inefficiencies that persisted in the public service (Ifill 2002).

---

[28] The Public Service Commission 2016 Annual Report highlights that the Public Service Commission filled 3,283 vacancies in the public service in 2016 (PSC 2016).

Table 4.03: Attempts to Reform the Public Service

Period	Reform description
1964	Reform programmes focused on terms and conditions for public servants
1970	Reform initiatives emphasised the improvement of institutional architecture and the restructuring of public service practices and procedures. Stakeholders expressed apprehension concerning over-centralization and inefficient disciplinary systems and performance appraisal systems
1973 - 1975	Implementation of the Administrative Improvement Programme. This initiative illuminated flaws in performance appraisals in addition to the need to provide better training opportunities for employees
1981	Effort to improve efficiency in the public service. Reform called for assignment in financial and personnel matters Main focus on job assessment, career development and training
1984 - 1986	Dumas Report – Review of Public Service Task Force. The assessment identified a need to improve the appraisal system across the public service
1989	Administrative Reform Programme. This programme reinforced the need for institutional strengthening. Key elements: formation of mission statements and development of strategic plans; improvement of organisational structures and processes; improve the financial management system
1992	Draper Report: Transform and improve the human relations management function in the public service
2007	Vision 2020: National Readiness Assessment Study. An integrated and holistic approach to national development initiatives

Source: Commonwealth Secretariat (2016)

4.4.2 Contract Labour in the Public Service

As previously mentioned, the inefficiency in the public service (in T&T, Guyana, and Suriname) causes long delays in the hiring process. Moreover, the lack of effective succession planning often results in workers retiring, and leaving with institutional knowledge. Vacancies created are not immediately filled, resulting in thousands of vacancies in the public service.

A report by the Joint Select Committee on Social Services and Public Administration notes that contract labour is frequently used to fill public sector vacancies in T&T. The report also highlights that there are two categories of contract workers in the public service in T&T.

> *"Contract employees employed to support the operations of Departments, Units and Divisions of Ministries.*
>
> *Political appointees - Cabinet approved contract positions for staff assigned to a Minister. A Minister has sole discretion to hire, discipline and when necessary terminate political appointees"* (PRTT 2018, 3).

Apart from the aforementioned contract workers, whose contract of employment tends to range from 1 year to 3 years, Permanent Secretaries of ministries also have the authority to hire people on short-term (3 to 6 months) contracts.

In December 2006, the GORTT developed the Government Human Resource Services Company Limited (GHRS), an employment agency to assist in the hiring of contract labour for the public service (GHRS 2014). The GHRS allowed people to apply for vacancies in the public service online, undertake an interview, and then obtain employment in the public service on contract. Although the GHRS was closed in 2017 (GORTT MPAC 2017), its employment system was faster than the service commissions.

At the end of the GHRS tenure, the Ministry of Labour launched the National Employment Service (NES), to advertise contract positions in the public service. From 2017 onwards, ministries proceed to interview and hire contract labour directly. Thus, there were 13,800 people employed on contract within various ministries and departments by the end of 2018.

As previously mentioned, the service commissions have the authority to appoint, promote, transfer and exercise disciplinary control over public officers. However, the service commissions do not have jurisdiction over contract labour in the public service. The Constitution of Trinidad and Tobago in Section 3 (4) (c) specifically states contract workers are not public officers

> *"(4) For the purposes of this Constitution a person shall not be considered to hold an office in the public service by reason only that—*

(c) he is—

(ii) a person appointed on contract for a period not exceeding five years" (LTT 1976, 15-16).

Nevertheless, the contract workers receive their official contract of service which states all their terms and conditions of employment from the Office of the Chief Personnel Officer (CPO).

In practice, some people may start with a 1-year or a 3-year contract of employment within a ministry. Workers whose contract of employment was for at least 1-year are eligible for a lump-sum gratuity payment, based on 25% of their gross salary over the contract period. Gratuity files for the contract workers are sent to the Treasury, and to the Auditor General Department for examination, which takes approximately 2 to 3 months to process.

Some workers that completed the contract of employment may have their contract renewed. This new contract comes from the Office of the CPO. In the interim, the Permanent Secretary may offer short-term contracts of employment to the workers to provide the workers with employment while the longer-term contract is being drafted by the CPO. In practice, the CPO can take years to process a contract of service, resulting in the worker employed for years in a ministry under a series of short-term contracts.

This short-term employment practice has several drawbacks for contract workers.

- The first drawback is it does not provide contract workers with job security, preventing them from obtaining long-term loans from financial institutions.
- The second drawback is the short-term contracts of service do not have a gratuity. Consequently, workers can spend over 3 years working under short-term contracts, but they would not receive a gratuity for each year of service.
- Third, the short-term contract workers do not receive the standard benefits (such as vacation leave, sick leave, a medical plan, etc.) which are offered to the permanent and long-term contract workers.
- Fourth, there are often delays in the processing of payments for the short-term contract workers.
- Fifth, in an attempt to break the service of contract workers, some short-term contract workers could be temporarily retrenched with no severance benefits for months before getting their contract renewed.

Guyana also relies upon contract labour in the public service. The system functions similar to T&T, where there are permanent workers that are hired through the service commissions, working alongside labour hired on fixed-term contracts directly by respective ministries. Contract labour is used as this system facilitates the faster filling of vacancies than the public service, and it allows for the hiring of workers with academic training and experience which may be difficult to obtain through the service commission system. Additionally, contract labour typically receives a higher nominal salary than the permanent workers, as well as a gratuity at the end of their fixed-term contract.

The contract workers in Guyana face similar challenges. The first limitation is that contract labour is placed in a weakened position of workers to negotiate for better terms and conditions of employment as an individual rather than as a bargaining unit of a trade union. The second limitation is the lack of job security of contract employment. Un-favoured workers can find themselves in a position where their contract is not renewed when it ends. This feeds into a third limitation, where contract labour may find difficulty in obtaining long-term loans and mortgages.

In Suriname, fixed-term contract labour is also used to fill vacancies in the public service. Belfor (2006) notes that the contract labour in Suriname is classified as follows:

- People working on fixed-term employment contracts;
- People working for a labour broker (contractor);
- Job contracting (contract for service);
- Labour only contracting;
- People employed temporarily by employment agencies.

Inefficiencies in government bureaucracy, as well as outdated labour laws account for the use of contract labour in the public service in Suriname. However, in practice, the social protection offered to contract labour is lower than that offered to permanent workers. The trade union membership among the contract workers is low, and the contract workers are in a weaker position to negotiate terms and conditions of employment with their employers than unionised workers (Belfor 2006).

The International Labour Organisation (ILO) has recognised this global rise in contract employment. The ILO asserts

> *"Among countries with available data, covering 84 per cent of total global employment, only around one-quarter (26.4 per cent) of workers are employed on a permanent contract, with around 13 per cent on a temporary or fixed-term contract and the significant majority (60.7 per cent) working without any contract"* (ILO 2015, 30).

The report goes on to state that the global shift from traditional employment relationships to more non-standard forms of employment and short-term contracts is causing employment relationships to become less secure (ILO 2015).

4.5 Inefficiency in the On-the-Job Training Programme

Private sector enterprises only consider the private cost and private benefits to inform decision-making. In the labour market, the private cost of the private sector enterprise would be the cost of training the young worker. The private benefit would be the increase in the productivity of the worker as they learn to perform their required duties. However, training carries public benefits as workers gain competence, their skills can be useful for other organisations. Furthermore, employment has significant positive externalities as it allows workers to financially provide for their families, and the expenditure of their salaries creates a multiplier effect to generate income for several other producers in the domestic value chains.

It is well noted in economics that the consideration of only the private costs and the private benefit can result in the underproduction of goods and services which have significant positive externalities (Lipsey and Chrystal 2003). This in turn results in market failure. In the labour market, the market failure is the presence of youth unemployment due to the reluctance of employers to train young workers. Fortunately, governments exist to correct these market failures.

In T&T, the government has long recognised that several of the nation's youth are unemployed because they are criticised for lacking "work experience". In 2002, the GORTT launched the On-the-Job Training (OJT) Programme, which provides apprenticeship opportunities for citizens of T&T between the ages of 16-35 (GORTT 2017). The objective of the programme is to help the young people in T&T gain work experience so that they can become more employable.

As of May 31st, 2017, the On-the-Job Training Programme became a Division of the Ministry of Labour.[29] At present, the OJT Programme facilitates the placement of trainees in various public and private agencies for a maximum of twenty-four months.

In principle, the OJT programme is good. However, the actual implementation of the programme is flawed. To help keep the unemployment rate suppressed at around 5%, the GORTT uses its OJT programme to create employment for young people. Several young people enrolled in the OJT programme are often allocated in ministries, and government organisations and placed in positions that do not utilise any of the skills that they acquired during their educational programme. This often results in situations where the young people gain work experience that is not aligned with their education and qualifications.

Notably, the GORTT will not be able to provide the appropriate work experience for every young graduate. This is because the government ministries and agencies perform mainly administrative duties, subsequently, workers are required to perform mainly administrative functions. In contrast, young graduates that pursued highly specialised educational training, (for example, graduates of physics, chemistry, actuarial science, etc.) will not receive the work experience that is aligned with their educational training.

In a sense, this OJT placement problem is a direct result of the GATE programme being not targeted at specific skill sets. The untargeted GATE encourages nationals of T&T to pursue education in any area of their choice. However, at the end of their programme, there may be no job in the country that could utilise the skills that they learned at the educational institution. This is a problem that is very common among the nationals of T&T that pursue tertiary education under GATE. In contrast, this problem is relatively non-existent among the nationals that pursue technical vocational training.

---

[29] The Cabinet of the GORTT agreed by Minute No. 496 dated March 21, 2002, to implement the OJT programme under the Ministry of Science, Technology and Tertiary Education with effect from April 1, 2002. The programme remained directly under the Ministry of Science until 2008. The Cabinet of the GORTT agreed by Minute No. 736 dated March 27, 2008, to transfer the administrative responsibility of the OJT programme to the National Training Agency (NTA). Gazette No. 125, Vol. 54, dated December 4, 2015 documented the transfer of the administrative responsibility of the OJT programme from the NTA to the Ministry of Labour (GORTT 2017).

Another limitation of the OJT programme is the quality of experience. Young workers allocated to various ministries and government agencies are not always placed in a learning environment. There are several instances where the on-the-job trainees go to work to do nothing. Therefore, after 24 months of acquiring work experience, the young worker may have gained no additional skills or competencies to help them perform work at a future job.

4.6 Summary Insight

T&T, Guyana, and Suriname are all vulnerable to macroeconomic shocks. Negative shocks can cause a significant decline in economic activity, and subsequently, give rise to unemployment in these economies.

Other shared reasons for unemployment in these countries are the outdated education systems which in turn do not produce graduates that are properly prepared for the world of work, and the inefficiency in the service commission hiring. T&T's experience with subsidised tertiary education has created additional problems, namely the excess supply of skilled labour, and the inefficient operation of an On-the-Job Training Programme.

While external macroeconomic shocks are beyond the control of any CARICOM government, policies can be implemented at the local level to improve the education and employment system. Moreover, the education system can be augmented to suit the labour needs and entrepreneurship opportunities for each country. This would involve the interaction between several stakeholders. The next chapter examines the various stakeholders that will be required to institute reforms to improve the education – labour – entrepreneurship system.

CHAPTER FIVE

STAKEHOLDERS AND REQUIRED INSTITUTIONAL FRAMEWORK FOR EMPLOYMENT CREATION

An appropriate enabling environment is required for employment creation. A policy framework is required to create sufficient income-earning opportunities for the citizens of the hydrocarbon-rich CARICOM Member States, reduce the friction and rigidity in employment,[30] equip the workforce with vital skills, and protect the rights of workers at the workplace.

Several stakeholders will be responsible for the creation of this enabling environment. These stakeholders include the government, public sector institutions, private sector institutions, non-government institutions, international institutions, and a new coordinating body to ensure the effective implementation of the enabling environment.

5.1 The Government

As mentioned in Chapter Three, the governments in the respective hydrocarbon-rich CARICOM Member States act as the lead employer in their respective countries. While it is admirable that the governments can directly or indirectly provide employment, the sole responsibility of employment should not reside with the government. The government's role is to use laws and policies to help create a society where no one is left behind.

In a full free-market economy, economic agents pursue actions to make and maximise profits. They consider only the private costs and benefits of production to inform their decisions. However, many goods and services generate externalities, as their production process affects several economic

[30] In other words, there should be a better labour market. Workers with the appropriate skills should be able to attain employment and income earning opportunities without facing nepotism, or any form of discrimination.

agents that were not directly responsible or involved in the production. Externalities give rise to public costs and public benefits. The public costs occur where there are negative externalities, while public benefits occur where there are positive externalities. The ignoring of the public costs can result in the overproduction of some goods, in comparison, the ignoring of the public benefits can result in the underproduction of other goods. These scenarios of overproduction and underproduction are market failures as the optimal output is not produced.

The government exists to correct these market failures. Several goods carry widespread economic benefits to society. However, they will not be provided by the private sector since they are non-excludable[31] in supply. Due to the non-excludable aspect of these goods, the private sector cannot charge a price for the provision of these goods and services, and thus they would not profit from these goods. These goods are referred to as public goods.

Other goods are excludable and carry large public benefits, however, if the private sector was left alone to provide these goods, too little of the goods would be available. These goods are referred to as merit goods.

Education and training are merit goods. The private sector can provide these goods. However, if the private sector was left alone to provide these goods, they would charge a high price for education, resulting in education being inaccessible to many people. Likewise, job training can also be provided by the private sector. However, the private sector tends to have a reluctance to train young workers, and possess the desire to free-ride and benefit from the training and gradual acquired competence of experienced workers. This unwillingness to provide training often prevents several young workers from gaining employment.

Another type of market failure which could occur is the exploitation of workers. Employers and owners of capital seek to maximise their return on their capital, while individual workers, who can be replaced, tend to have less negotiating power than their employers. Furthermore, several unethical people often rise to managerial positions. Consequently, management personnel sometimes do not always act in good faith or in the best interest of workers. Hence governments are needed to correct these labour market

[31] Non-excludability means that once a good is provided, the provider cannot prevent other economic agents from benefiting from it. An example of a non-excludable good is a street light. Once a streetlight is providing illumination, everyone in the vicinity of the streetlight would benefit from it.

failures by passing industrial relations laws and implementing labour policies.

The Role of Government as A Regulator

The governments of the hydrocarbon-rich CARICOM Member States are responsible for making laws that provide social protection for their citizens. Unfortunately, the labour laws (in T&T, Guyana, and Suriname) are outdated and do not cover the wide spectrum of industrial relations issues in the present era. There is a need for all the aforementioned acts to be reviewed, and based on stakeholder consultations, revised to reflect the more modern times.

Some of the reforms that are needed to amend the labour laws include:

- The need for a labour law to make any provision for redress of workers who have been refused employment due to biased recruitment procedures by the employer.
- The need for a labour law to prioritise the compensation of workers if an employer files for bankruptcy.
- The need for a labour law to broaden the definition of a worker. Presently, trainees and domestic workers are not recognised as workers in the existing labour legislations. Consequently, these unrecognised workers cannot legally seek any redress through the Industrial Court for any rights dispute.
- The need for a labour law to mandate that retired workers, or workers that have provided years of service to an employer should receive a gratuity upon retirement.
- The need for a labour law to provide minimum levels of overtime payment for all categories of workers. Presently the minimum wages order sets the overtime payment, but the provisions are only applicable to workers whose wages reside in the minimum wage range.
- The need for a labour law to mandate employers to provide a minimum level of health coverage for workers. Several workers are employed and have no health insurance plan, and no pension plan.
- The need for a labour law to address the vulnerabilities of contract labour. Presently, no law mandates that an employer must rehire a contract worker, if they have demonstrated both competence and good working ethics at the workplace. Subsequently, the contract

renewal process can be very subjective, and unrelated to the performance of the worker.

- The need for a labour law to create a comprehensive system to protect "whistleblowers" reporting corruption and wrongdoing in the workplace.
- The need for a labour law to protect workers from sexual harassment.

5.2 Public Institutions

Several public institutions have a key role in the labour market in the hydrocarbon-rich CARICOM Member States. Currently, the service commissions play a significant role in generating employment opportunities in the countries. However, if the Governments of T&T, Guyana, and Suriname aspire to encourage more entrepreneurship, their educational institutions should be a central focal point to stimulate the change. This approach was considered by Nigeria, Malaysia, and Singapore as they tried to produce more graduate entrepreneurs.

The Role of the Educational Institutions

The education system in T&T, Guyana, and Suriname continues to be shaped by their colonial past. During the colonial era, slaves and ex-slaves were educated through the work of missionaries. Therefore, religion played an important role in developing education in the hydrocarbon-rich CARICOM Member States, resulting in the formation of the denominational primary and secondary schools (Campbell 1992; James 2013).

Each country (T&T, Guyana, and Suriname) has a mandate for children to undergo primary and secondary education. At the end of Form 5, students are required to write Ordinary Level (O-Level) examinations, the Caribbean Secondary Education Certificate (CSEC), or the Caribbean Examination Council (CXC), which tests their knowledge on various subjects. Students earning passes at the CXC may proceed on to the Advanced Level (A-Level), where they may continue their studies in 4 subjects, and then sit the Cambridge School Certificate A-Level examinations, or the Caribbean Advanced Proficiency Examination (CAPE). Students successful at the A-Level may proceed to a tertiary education where they may study for an undergraduate degree. The University of the West Indies is an option for tertiary education for many A-Level graduates, as it requires good scores at the A-Levels examinations to grant students entry. Prior to the Dollar for Dollar programme and the GATE programme, only the students that could have afforded to pay tuition fees, or the students that took student loans would have pursued tertiary education in the private institutions. However, after the implementation of GATE, there was an increase in tertiary enrollment at all the tertiary educational institutions in T&T.

The academic system (O-Levels, A-Levels, and degrees) mirrors the British education system. This system places heavy emphasis on exams, rote learning, regurgitation, and conformity of thought. It is noteworthy that except for basic Math and English, the information acquired at the O-Level and the A-Level is useless in helping any individual become a SME. In many cases, the information acquired at the undergraduate degree level does not give a university graduate any advantage in starting a business over an individual that did not receive flamboyant results at the O-Level. Individuals without high passes at the O-Level are more likely to become SMEs, whereas individuals with the degree qualifications are likely to look for a job in the formal sector.

Some students may opt to pursue training in technical vocational areas after completing form 5. Technical and vocational education and training (TVET) is a comprehensive term referring to those aspects of the education process involving the study of technologies and related sciences, and acquisition of practical skills, attitudes, understanding, and knowledge relating to occupants in various sectors of economic and social life. The objective of technical and vocational education is to help people to develop application-oriented competencies that have related technical theoretical knowledge and practical ability. The theoretical requirements for TVET are low, and more emphasis is placed on hands-on capacity. Moreover, it is geared towards the practical needs of heavy industries, and the real economy (Cong and Wang 2012).

In contrast to academic education which does not prepare young people for the world of work, TVET gives people useful skills which are applicable in many industries, and can empower people to become service-providing SMEs. To incorporate technical developments, there must be a collaboration between the TVET schools and the industries. The TVET teaching syllabus should be drafted to meet the needs of the industry. Students should be enrolled in a teaching curriculum that incorporates both classroom learning, as well as practical sessions. Additionally, practitioners from the industry should also be invited to teach and supervise educational sessions to help facilitate learning (Cong and Wang 2012).

One study recognises the importance of TVET

> *"The role of technical and vocational education and training in this process is key, especially as the global and regional economy undergoes significant changes. The world of work is evolving rapidly, as productive structures adapt to the shifts induced by the emergence of new technologies and new business models. Skills in this environment tend to depreciate quickly and therefore must be continually updated. In this sense, TVET provides opportunities to transition students into this new world of work as well as keeping existing workers employed. TVET targeted at women, youth, senior citizens and other vulnerable populations also provides governments with significant leverage to reduce inequality and poverty"* (Hanni 2019, 11).

It is noteworthy that TVET has been recognised as a working strategy that contributes to increasing efficiency in education investment. Moreover, countries (such as China, Iraq, Ghana, South Africa, Vietnam) seeking to excel in international trade and survive global competition are undertaking reforms on their education and training systems to develop the required skills-based workforce (Allais 2012; Boateng 2012; Cong and Wang 2012; Constant et al. 2014; Wrana and Nguyen 2019).

One study asserts

> *"The development of technical and vocational education and training has become one of the important strategies of education development in both developing and developed countries. In the international community, where education in general is concerned, the rates-of-return analyses suggest that the economic payoff to education is high and remains sizable with economic growth"* (Tabbron and Yang 1997, 323).

Given that TVET has significant potential, the policy makers in the hydrocarbon-rich CARICOM Member States should encourage technical vocational training. This can be achieved through:

1. The reform of the secondary school system, where the schools' curriculum is expanded to include all the technical vocational areas.
2. The development of more TVET institutions, especially in Guyana and Suriname, to train students after they have completed form 5.
3. The encouragement of young people to pursue technical vocational training offered at the existing institutions.
4. Creating a financial incentive to encourage young people that completed form 5 to pursue technical vocational training rather than academic studies. For example, a small stipend could be offered to the students.
5. Providing career guidance to young people to pursue technical vocational training. The young people should be advised about the

wide range of employment opportunities, and income-earning capabilities from TVET, and the potential difficulty they could be facing in gaining employment when they pursue academic programmes.

6. Amending the subsidisation of post-secondary education to encourage TVET rather than academic studies. This can be done by offering full subsidisation of tuition for the TVET, while partial subsidisation can be provided for academic studies based on a means test.
7. Restructure all the TVET programmes, so that after completing form 5, students may start a programme, upon completion the students may earn a degree rather than a certificate or diploma.
8. Develop a comprehensive business incubation programme comprising 3 phases. In the first phase, the young people are enrolled in a TVET programme. In the second phase, the student is enrolled as a trainee on a jobsite to acquire work experience. In the third phase, the graduate is provided with a loan which they may use to purchase tools and equipment to start a business. During the first year of operation, the student may work with a mentor to supervise their business operations to ensure their viability.

5.3 The Private Sector

The private sector presently plays a huge role in facilitating economic activity in the hydrocarbon-rich CARICOM Member States. This is evidenced by the private sector mobilising the necessary financial and physical capital to engage in exploration and production activity in the countries. The sustained growth of the economies (T&T, Guyana, and Suriname) is presently dependent on the ability and capacity of private enterprises to pursue market opportunities effectively, and in the presence of the appropriate fiscal frameworks.

Foreign multinational companies dominate production in the hydrocarbon sector in the countries. Hydrocarbon exports account for approximately 80% of exports in T&T, and are expected to acquire the lion share of exports in Guyana and Suriname as they monetize the hydrocarbon deposits from the Guyana-Suriname basin.

The hydrocarbon value chain is composed of three segments:

- upstream – exploration and production;
- midstream – transportation and processing; and
- downstream – marketing and distribution.

Generally, the foreign multinational companies operating in the hydrocarbon value chain in T&T, Guyana, and Suriname are vertically integrated, and can provide all the services that they require. Nevertheless, there is scope to outsource some of these services and functions to local stakeholders. This can be achieved through the implementation of a local content policy, which would allow local stakeholders to acquire a greater share of the value-added from the hydrocarbon value chain. This effectively strengthens the backward and forward linkages between the hydrocarbon sector and the other sectors of the economies. Table 5.1 provides a summary of the various opportunities.

Table 5.1: Opportunities in the Hydrocarbon Value Chain

Upstream (Exploration & Production)	Mid-stream (Refining)	Downstream (Sale of Final Product to Market)
Technical	Technical	Technical
Chemical Engineering	Chemical Engineering	
Mechanical Engineering	Mechanical Engineering	
Electrical Engineering	Electrical Engineering	
Instrumentation	Instrumentation	
Operations / Production	Operations / Production	
Piping Engineering	Piping Engineering	
Petroleum Engineering	Petroleum Engineering	
Process Engineering	Process Engineering	
Subsea Engineering		
QA / QC / Inspection		
Structural Engineering		
Field Telecommunications		
Wireline Field Operations		
Diving		
Underwater Welding		
Wells and Xmas Tree Engineering		
Process Engineering		
Project Controls		
Drilling		
Platform Fabrication		
Well Logging		
Geophysics		
Geochemistry		
Marine biology		

Mud Logging		
Hydrographic Surveying		
Aerial Surveying		
Semi-Technical	Semi-Technical	Semi-Technical
Economic Evaluation and Market Research	Economic Evaluation and Market Research	Economic Evaluation and Market Research
Marketing and Promotion	Marketing and Promotion	Marketing and Promotion
Legal	Legal	Legal
Health and Safety	Health and Safety	Health and Safety
Accounting	Accounting	Accounting
Tax Administration	Tax Administration	Tax Administration
Information Technology	Information Technology	Information Technology
Navigation		
Compliance		
Non-Technical		
Materials / Logistics / Stores	Materials / Logistics / Stores	Materials / Logistics / Stores
Tent and Equipment Rentals	Tent and Equipment Rentals	Tent and Equipment Rentals
Administration	Administration	Administration
Food and catering sales	Food and catering sales	Food and catering sales
Janitorial	Janitorial	Janitorial
Public Relations/ Communication	Public Relations/ Communication	Public Relations/ Communication
Purchasing	Purchasing	Purchasing
Security	Security	Security
Driving	Driving	Driving
		Hotel and Guest House Accommodation

The technical services can be provided by local stakeholders in T&T. This is possible due to T&T's long history in the hydrocarbon industry, which has allowed it to develop multiple technical schools, programmes, and train its labour force to develop the required skills. In contrast, Guyana and Suriname are on the eve of their hydrocarbon boom, and will take several years to develop the required skilled labour force.

Nevertheless, there is scope for all countries (T&T, Guyana, and Suriname) to provide semi-technical and non-technical services for the foreign multinational hydrocarbon companies operating in their respective country.

Notably, as multinationals seek to maximise profits, there may be a tendency for the multinationals to use very little local inputs and support services in the hydrocarbon sector. This can be addressed through the development of a local content policy, which mandates that locals should be given preference in the supply of local inputs and support services once they have the capacity.

T&T presently has a local policy, but as it was drafted in 2004, it is outdated and does not effectively guarantee preference is provided to locals. This deficiency was partially corrected by the government in 2006 through its introduction of local content requirements in the production sharing contracts (PSCs) for the hydrocarbon sector.

In December 2021, Guyana passed its local content bill, which outlines 40 services that hydrocarbon companies and their subcontractors must procure from Guyanese producers. The local content requirements percentages range from 5% for engineering and technical maintenance to as much as 100% for administration support services (Palmigiani 2022).

The Government of Suriname also recognises the importance of local content policy in helping local stakeholders earn a greater share of the value-added from their hydrocarbon industry. Subsequently, by the end of 2021, it was in the process of developing a local content policy for its hydrocarbon industry.

5.4 Other Non-Government Actors

There are several non-governmental stakeholders involved in the labour market in T&T, Guyana, and Suriname. The notable ones include trade unions, and international organisations.

The Role of Trade Unions

A trade union is an organisation, which is typically composed of workers, which have been formed to represent and negotiate on the behalf of the interest and welfare of workers.

In the nineteenth century, many academics and international institutions viewed trade unions in a negative light. Trade unions were blamed for increasing the costs of labour, decreasing the cost competitiveness of firms, and contributing to inflation in economies (Oswalf 1985; Alesina and Perotti 1994; Siebert 1997). While some people hold this myopic view today, trade unions have contributed significantly to the improvement of working conditions, rights, and benefits of workers in all societies.

In T&T, Guyana, and Suriname, trade unions directly play a role in industrial relations with regards to rights disputes, and interest disputes. A rights dispute is a trade dispute between an employer and a worker regarding the rights of the worker on the job. Issues such as wrongful dismissal, unfair suspensions, a lack of procedural fairness, the denial of the opportunity to be heard, and the denial of any right of the worker at the jobsite all fall under the jurisdiction of rights disputes.

An interest dispute is a trade dispute between an employer and a specific bargaining unit of workers, regarding the terms and conditions of employment of the workers. Interest disputes involve the collective bargaining between the employer and the trade union representing the specific bargaining union. They cover issues such as the wages of workers, the hours of work, the compensation for overtime work, safety conditions, and other terms of employment of the workers.

Since the service commissions (in T&T, Guyana, and Suriname) are protected by the Constitution of each country, the service commissions are likely to stay for many years extending into the future. As the service commissions each have a trade union to represent specific bargaining units of workers, these trade unions are likely to remain relevant. There is likely to be a continuation of the dual employment process in the public service where some workers are hired permanently by a service commission, while others are hired by fixed-term contracts. As these trade unions attached to the public service organisation engage in collective bargaining every 3 years, the terms and conditions from their collective agreements are likely to act as a price floor or benchmark of the minimum terms and conditions that contract workers should receive.

The Role of the International Organisations

There are 2 international organisations whose principles and practices of industrial relations serve as a guide for industrial relations in the CARICOM Member States. The first is the International Labour Organisation (ILO), a tripartite United Nations (UN) agency that collaborates with governments, employers, and trade unions of 187 member States, to set labour standards, which parties agree are fair, humane, equitable, and facilitates decent work for all workers.

The second entity is the CARICOM Secretariat and its Declaration of Labour and Industrial Relations Principles. After Caribbean countries gained their independence from the United Kingdom, they each developed industrial relations legislation. However, these laws were fragmented. To harmonise labour legislation in the Caribbean, in April 1993, the Twelfth Meeting of the Standing Committee of Ministers of Labour (SCML), welcomed the proposal from the Special Meeting of the Working Party of Labour Officials for a Declaration of Labour and Industrial Relations Principles (CARICOM 2016). The Declaration sets out the principles of the industrial relations to which the CARICOM Region strives to adhere. It is noteworthy that the CARICOM Declaration of Labour and Industrial Relations Principles is based on the conventions from the ILO.

The Role of the ILO

The ILO conventions establish the basic principles and rights of a worker at work. Eight conventions have been identified as "fundamental", and essential rights of workers at work (ILO 2014). Table 5.2 outlines the fundamental conventions.

All 8 of the fundamental conventions have been ratified by the CARICOM Member States.

The sustained promotion of decent work in member states requires the national institutions in the member states to establish systems to ensure compliance with labour standards. Subsequently, the ILO developed governance conventions to assist in the labour administration in member states.

Given that the labour legislation in the CARICOM Member States is slow to change, the ILO Conventions and its principles are often used as a guide for industrial relations in each country. In moving forward, the ILO and its Conventions will continue to act as a benchmark to provide a direction as to what is fair and just industrial relations principles in the hydrocarbon-rich CARICOM Member States.

Table 5.2: Fundamental Conventions of the ILO

Name of Convention	Principle established	Date Ratified by GORTT
C029 - Forced Labour Convention, 1930 (No. 29)	Prohibits the use of forced labour.	May 24, 1963
C087 - Freedom of Association and Protection of the Right to Organise Convention, 1948 (No. 87)	Establishes the right of workers to form organisations (trade unions), and engage in the organisation's duties.	May 24, 1963
C098 - Right to Organise and Collective Bargaining Convention, 1949 (No. 98)	Establishes the right of workers to engage in collective bargaining with employers.	May 24,1963
C100 - Equal Remuneration Convention, 1951 (No. 100)	Establishes the right of equal remuneration for men and women workers for work of equal value.	May 29, 1997
C105 - Abolition of Forced Labour Convention, 1957 (No. 105)	Mandates that member states which ratified this convention, take effective measures to completely abolish forced labour.	May 24, 1963
C111 - Discrimination (Employment and Occupation) Convention, 1958 (No. 111)	Prohibits discrimination based on a person's physical characteristics at the work place.	Nov 26, 1970
C138 - Minimum Age Convention, 1973 (No. 138)	It establishes the minimum age for employment to be 18 years.	Sep 03, 2004
C182 - Worst Forms of Child Labour Convention, 1999 (No. 182)	It prohibits child labour, the sale and trafficking of children, debt bondage, child prostitution, and using a child for illicit activities.	Apr 23, 2003

Source: ILO (2014)

5.5 Implementation and Coordination Project Steering Committee

To drive the transformation process where the appropriate enabling environment for employment creation is generated, an entity will have to be delegated with the corresponding responsibility. To this end, a project steering committee should be formed to coordinate the project's implementation.

This project steering committee should be a tripartite body comprised of representatives from:

i) The ministry of labour - since employment creation affects the labour force. Furthermore, this ministry is responsible for the administration of labour relations in the respective CARICOM Member States.
ii) The ministry of trade and industry - since the project would aspire to strengthen the backward and forward linkages between industries in countries, and should also aspire to help SMEs engage in trade.
iii) The private sector – since the private sector currently engages in business activities and are aware of all the challenges in doing business and exporting goods and services.
iv) The tertiary and technical vocational education body – since the educational institutions produce graduates which eventually enter the labour force. There needs to be greater collaboration and communication between the educational institutions and the industry to ensure that the educational institutions produce graduates with the correct skills which are demanded by the labour market, or skills that the graduates could commercialise into business activities.
v) The trade union movement – since they represent the rights and interests of workers. Input from the trade union movement would also be essential in promoting a harmonious industrial relations climate.
vi) The ILO – since this international organisation collaborates with the international community to agree upon what is fair and just industrial relations practices.

At the project steering committee's inception, it should develop an action plan, which would itemise all the activities they intend to coordinate for the fiscal year. The plan should indicate:

- the activities/workshop involved in the promotion of entrepreneurship education in the respective countries;
- the activities for the training of citizens of the respective CARICOM Member States in the business entrepreneurship programme;
- the activities involved in the pooling of finance for the SMEs in the business entrepreneurship programme;

- the activities involved in building the capacity of SMEs to help them export;
- the identification of markets for exports for the SMEs that have upgraded in capacity;
- the activities involved in the building of networks (domestically and regionally) to help the professional export their services;
- the activities involved in developing an e-commerce platform; and
- the activities involved in creating the policy and legal framework to support e-commerce.

The action plan should also include a logical framework, which connects measurable objectives to activities, as well as timelines for the achievement of the goals. This can be complemented by annual monitoring and evaluation, to track the committee's progress in achieving its deliverables.

The monitoring and evaluation system should:

- include the monitoring of inputs, including resource allocation, total costs, and project expenditure;
- monitor the processes and outputs;
- evaluate the outcomes;
- identify deficiencies, which could be later corrected;
- facilitate an effective feedback mechanism that makes statistical information available in a useable form to the government, and other relevant stakeholders;
- help reinforce the institutional arrangements; and
- eventually evolve into an efficient system for generating relevant, reliable, and timely quantitative and qualitative disaggregated information.

5.6 Summary Insight

The ideal enabling environment for the promotion of entrepreneurship will involve several actors. The first stakeholder will be the government, as it is responsible for creating laws and policies, which can favourably impact entrepreneurs.

The second stakeholder is the educational institutions, which will be key to training people and equipping them with the required skills to develop a business.

The third stakeholder is the private sector. The hydrocarbon-rich CARICOM Member States are very fortunate to possess their hydrocarbon industries, as it presents a multitude of opportunities for entrepreneurs to supply support services to the larger private-sector corporations. Backward linkages can be strengthened to supply support services in the upstream sector, and forward linkages can be developed as the hydrocarbon inputs can be processed into downstream products.

The fourth stakeholder includes non-governmental institutions such as the trade unions and the ILO. These institutions will be essential in producing a labour market that adheres to the principles and practices of good industrial relations.

The fifth stakeholder is a proposed Implementation and Coordination Project Steering Committee. This project steering committee should be a tripartite body that is responsible for driving the entrepreneurship transformation process. This project steering committee will be essential in encouraging a healthy and dynamic business sector, and introducing specific interventions to improve the competitiveness, productivity, and export capability of SMEs.

The next chapter explores the areas for potential opportunities for entrepreneurship and employment creation in the hydrocarbon-rich CARICOM Member States. This can help develop a greater understanding of where growth can emerge and higher-productivity employment opportunities can be created.

CHAPTER SIX

IDENTIFYING POTENTIAL SECTORS FOR EMPLOYMENT CREATION

Recall, there is a large cohort of young people in the hydrocarbon-rich CARICOM Member States that are without work.[32] Faced with large labour surpluses, the governments should be interested in exploring investment areas that will absorb labour to facilitate production and generate inclusive economic growth.[33]

Indeed, the GORTT have faced this challenge before in the 1980s, and responded with industrial policy. More specifically, the GORTT diversified T&T's economy by venturing into the natural gas, and downstream natural gas industries. This resulted in the creation of several industrial estates (industrial parks) in T&T (Boopsingh and McGuire 2004). The most notable ones are the Point Lisas and the Point-a-Pierre industrial estates.

Certainly, the industrial estate model is a success in T&T. It encouraged the private sector to venture into several business opportunities in T&T, subsequently generating employment for people residing in the host communities. Moreover, this model also creates positive multiplier effects as entrepreneurs that are not directly employed in the industrial estate also benefit when the industrial estate workers purchase their goods and services.

In facing this new employment challenge, the GORTT could once again respond with industrial policy. In contrast to the industrialization that occurred in the 1990s, natural gas-based industrialization may not be

---

[32] Although T&T's unemployment rate was 4.8% in 2017, there were approximately 32.6 thousand people officially unemployed. Furthermore, there were 437 thousand non-institutionalised people without jobs the same year. Since these non-institutionalised people are not part of the labour force, they are likely to be discouraged workers who are not actively seeking employment, but they would like to be employed.

[33] Inclusive economic growth is growth that occurs amid productivity improvements and the creation of new employment opportunities.

possible in the immediate future in T&T. This is a consequence of the country facing natural gas curtailment issues.[34]

Following the doctrine of Arthur Lewis, one may think that FDI in heavy industries may be the answer.[35] However, heavy industries are capital intensive, and employ a small percentage of the labour force. This highlights a need to rethink the approach in using foreign capital to stimulate commerce and entrepreneurship in a small economy.

Singapore is one of the few indisputable success stories that show what has to be done to promote innovation, research, and entrepreneurship. The success of Singapore in stimulating innovation reflects that when a domestic market is small, high-value services should be global-centric through mobilisation into foreign markets from the start (Ng 2015). Success can also be built through leveraging foreign capital, technology, and talent. However, it should be properly coordinated by the government and its state-owned institutions to encourage the spillover of physical capital, financial capital, technological knowledge, and marketing strategies to the locals. This is done to generate opportunities mainly in labour-intensive industries as these industries present greater scope for employment creation. Furthermore, the innovation and entrepreneurship system can be managed as an effective macroeconomic blend of efforts by the private sector, academia, and the government.

---

[34] Natural gas production in T&T declined from 4.2 Bcf/d in 2013, to 3.3 Bcf/d in 2016. Natural gas production may average 3.5 Bcf/d in 2020.

[35] Lewis (1954) envisaged industrialization as a process requiring the simultaneous development of agriculture and industry. Lewis begins by simplifying an economy to one with only 2 sectors: an agriculture sector, and an industrial sector. In such a model, economic growth is achieved by restructuring the economy to become more industrial based. Labour is assumed to be perfectly mobile, and thus should move the agricultural sector, to the industrial sector. A key feature of Lewis model is the recommendation for workers to be continued to be paid a subsistence wage. This subsistence wage strategy allows investors to earn profits, which can be reinvested. Reinvested profits can gradually allow for the increase in employment in the economy. Subsequently, the surplus labour in the economy is gradually absorbed.

In countries where the industrial sector was not present initially, the government should, through a series of policy measures, court foreign entrepreneurs to install and open their businesses. Hence the popular term, “industrialization by invitation”. The attracting of foreign investment could also contribute to spillover of fundamental technical, managerial, and entrepreneurial skills that may be initially absent in the home country.

An econometric analysis was performed on the impact of services and manufacturing on the real GDP growth in T&T. The details are expressed in the Appendix. The results of a Vector Error Correction Model (VECM) and its corresponding variance decomposition indicate that services **may have a greater contribution to T&T's economy than manufacturing.** These results are consistent with the findings in the literature that indicate services and labour intensive industries can make large contributions to economies (Loh Rahim et al. 2015; Nawawi et al. 2020; Nawaz and Koc 2020). Subsequently, the econometric findings provide justification for the GORTT to emphasise the development of services as it has great potential to contribute positively to T&T's economy. The empirical findings can also be extended for the policy direction of Guyana, and Suriname.

The following sections would review the potential labour-intensive industries which could create employment opportunities.

6.1 Export of Education

Globally, there are thousands of universities in the world offering training in a multitude of academic disciplines. The top universities and tertiary educational institutions are often found in developed countries, and emerging economies. These universities typically require a student to possess high scores on various examinations to gain acceptance and enrolment. For example, in the United States (US), the Scholastic Assessment Test (SAT) is used for college undergraduate admissions. For post-graduate admissions, universities in the US and Canada use the Graduate Record Examinations (GRE). In the United Kingdom (UK), the Cambridge International General Certificate of Education: Advanced Level, also known as Cambridge GCE A-Levels, is used for college undergraduate admissions. Students are required to gain high scores in these admissions tests to gain acceptance into the top universities. Unfortunately, not all students seeking admission will make the required scores on the entrance examinations.

There is a demand for tertiary education by students, however, the admissions examination tests render the supply inaccessible for many students. This excess demand for tertiary education creates an opportunity. Entrepreneurs that can supply the demanded tertiary education can capitalise on this demand. This gives rise to the offshore education industry.

Offshore educational institutions are educational institutions established in a home country to grant recognised certification (academic degrees or technical vocational qualifications) to foreign students (Wang 2017).

Offshore educational institutions are distinct from traditional local educational institutions. The notable differences include:

i. Offshore educational institutions target foreign students. Therefore, the student population of an offshore educational institution is predominantly of foreign students rather than locals of the host country.
ii. The curriculum of the offshore educational institutions matches the curriculum offered in the foreign country. For example, offshore Canadian universities operating in China and Australia offer Canadian-based curriculums.
iii. Offshore educational institutions are typically for-profit, private sector institutions. In contrast, several traditional universities do not operate with the profit-maximising mandate.

The 'offshoring' education is proliferating for several reasons. First, the global competition among educational institutions for students is an incentive for schools to attract foreign students. Second, the ease with which entrepreneurs may establish an offshore educational institution in a home country favours their development. For example, in some countries in the Caribbean, a business licence is the only requirement to establish an offshore medical university. In contrast, in the US, entrepreneurs must undergo rigorous assessment criteria to establish an accredited university (Parolini and Platek 2010; Babcock et al. 2013). The third reason is the increasing demand from families for tertiary education globally fuels the market for international education (Wang 2017).

There are four channels in which a home country can capture value from the export of education services.

i. The first channel is the cross-border supply of education services, where a local provider located in the home country provides education services to foreign students.
ii. The second channel is the onshore consumption of education by foreign students. This includes their expenditure on fees to the educational institution, as well as expenditure on various consumer goods and services in the host country, such as rent, food, clothing, travelling, and entertainment.

iii. The third channel is the offshore provision of international education, such as when a local educational institution sets up a campus overseas. As the foreign student must pay tuition, this results in factor incomes from abroad (FIFA) returning to the home country of the university.
iv. The fourth channel is the temporary allocation of local educators to foreign institutions overseas for a period under 12 months for the provision of education services. This includes guest lectures and fly-in quality assurance checks. The lecturers from the home country benefit when they receive their salaries while lecturing abroad.

The export of education (both academic and technical vocational) is a recommended strategy to be pursued in the hydrocarbon-rich CARICOM Member States as it can generate foreign exchange from the foreigners that enroll in these programmes locally. Certainly, the increase in enrollment can benefit local universities as they have expressed that they are experiencing financial difficulty (Bridglal 2017, Dowlat-Rostant 2019).

Furthermore, offshore education is attractive as it generates teaching employment opportunities for the people that pursued highly specialised training but are unable to find employment opportunities in their country.

While the export of education is recommended as a labour-intensive industry to provide employment, the industry is not new to the Caribbean. In fact, since the 1970s, offshore medical universities have been operating in the Caribbean (McLean and Charles 2018).

In T&T, several tertiary education institutions are offering offshore programmes. For instance, the School of Business and Computer Science (SBCS) offers degree programmes from universities whose head offices are in the US, Canada, and Europe. The School of Accounting and Management (SAM) offers degree programmes from the Anglia Ruskin University, whose head office is in the UK. SITAL College of Tertiary Education Limited offers degree programmes from the University of Hertfordshire, whose head office is also located in the UK.

Guyana also has several foreign institutions offering offshore programmes. The offshore medical universities include:

- American International School of Medicine;
- Georgetown American University;
- Green Heart Medical University;
- Lincoln American University;
- Rajiv Gandhi University of Science and Technology; and
- Texila American University.

Suriname also has several foreign educational institutions that target international students. The notable institutions include:

- Anton de Kom University of Suriname;
- Polytechnic College Suriname; and
- Academy for Higher Art and Culture Education.

Therefore, it would be rational for the governments of the respective countries to consider the export of education from all their tertiary educational institutions, not just the medical institutions.

6.2 Creative Industries

T&T, Guyana, and Suriname are havens for creative cultural products. The countries' creative sectors are multifaceted as multiple sub-sectors are existing within the country's creative sector. These creative sectors can be divided into the festivals, music, arts, fashion, and media services subsectors. The festival sub-sector comprises the Carnival festival, and various Carnival-type festivals. The music subsector includes the calypso, extempo, soca, chutney, and parang music genres. The arts sub-sector is comprised of performing arts (live music, theatre, film), visual arts (painting, sculptures, and art gallery), and handicrafts.

The subsectors of the creative industry are interrelated and complement each other. For instance, the Carnival industry creates revenue-earning opportunities for multiple stakeholders involved in the creative industry. Table 6.01 provides an overview.

Table 6.01: Potential Revenue Earning Opportunities from Carnival

Activities
Mass production and wire bending
Fetes
Food and beverage sales
Advertising and printing
Music composition and production
Royalties from music, and other media
Live performance (singing and dancing)
Domestic sales and export of steel pans
Media coverage
Accommodation
Car rentals
Inter-island transport (between Trinidad and Tobago)
Visitor expenditure in countries after Carnival
Intra-island visitor expenditure (e.g. to the beaches, parks, etc)
Souvenirs and handicrafts
Tents for camping
Transport (maxis and taxis)

Several large stakeholders directly benefit from the Carnival festival. For instance, the mass band producers directly benefit from Carnival as their mass costume products are sold to the general population. This directly creates employment opportunities for the people involved in mass production and its organisation.

Promoters and stakeholders involved in the organising of Carnival fetes also directly benefit, as there is an increase in fetes during the Carnival season.

Hotels and owners of resorts and guest houses benefit from the Carnival festival as it results in an increase in tourists' arrivals, and visitor stay-over.

Media organisations also benefit as they are often paid to broadcast Carnival activities, and advertise the products and services of various stakeholders.

Several small-scale stakeholders also benefit from the Carnival festival. Small and micro-entrepreneurs produce and sell food and beverages, handicrafts, clothes, and provide taxi services. As there is often an influx of thousands of people to the popular beaches during the Carnival weekend, SMEs providing goods and services at these areas also experience an increase in commerce.

The Carnival season can generate millions of dollars in total revenue in each country. Moreover, large-scale entrepreneurs, as well as SMEs, can benefit from the additional commerce generated from Carnival activities. For this reason, it would be rational for the governments of the countries to encourage the marketing and promoting of Carnival activities internationally. This can help market each country as a brand and help earn more foreign exchange for the countries.

6.3 Technical Vocational Services

Another labour-intensive industry that T&T, Guyana, and Suriname can participate in is the provision of technical vocational services. This area should be targeted especially by the hydrocarbon-rich CARICOM Member States as there is tremendous opportunity to develop and strengthen backward linkages.

The hydrocarbon sector relies on technical vocational services to facilitate production. Skills in electrical and electronics, mechanical, instrumentation, process operations, welding and fabrication, wood working, are very useful for the energy industry. Moreover, these technical-vocational skills are also attractive features as they can be used in SME business ventures. In other words, a person possessing the aforementioned skills does not need to rely on an employer to obtain a job. They can sell these services to the general population.

T&T, as the CARICOM Member State with the oldest hydrocarbon industry, had sufficient time to develop multiple technical-vocational institutions and programmes. For instance, there are state-owned agencies such as the National Energy Skills Centre (NESC), and the Youth Training and Employment Partnership Programme (YTEPP) which provide technical vocational training.

The NESC offers short courses in:

- Advanced Welding Levels 1 and 2;
- Air Conditioning and Refrigeration – Installation;
- Air Conditioning and Refrigeration – Maintenance;
- Air Conditioning and Refrigeration – Advanced Troubleshooting;
- Building Trade: Carpentry;
- Building Trade: Plumbing;
- Derrickman;
- Electrical Installation – Domestic;

- Electrical Installation – Commercial/Industrial;
- Heavy Equipment Operation (HEO);
- Industrial Mechanical Maintenance – Hydraulic and Pneumatics;
- Industrial Mechanical Maintenance – Hydraulics;
- Shielded Metal Arc Welding – Level 1; and
- Shielded Metal Arc Welding – Level 2.

1-year Craftsman certificates in:

- Plumbing; and
- Commercial Electrician.

2-year diplomas in:

- Welding;
- Electrical;
- Refrigeration and Air Conditioning;
- Information Technology Network Specialist;
- Automotive Services and Heavy Equipment Technician;
- Drilling Rig Operations; and
- Millwright.

All of the aforementioned programmes (short courses, 1-year certificate, and 2-year diploma) are demanded by the hydrocarbon sector, and have the potential to be developed into a business venture. Some of these skills can be used by the manufacturing sector, and the construction sector.

YTEPP offers (less than 1 year) courses in:

- Agro-Food Processing – Level 1;
- Air Conditioning and Refrigeration – Level 1;
- Cosmetology – Level 1;
- Data Operations – Level 1;
- Draughting and Construction Technician – Levels 1, 2, and 3;
- Editing and Advanced Camera Operations – Levels 1 and 2;
- Electrical Installation – Levels 1 and 2;
- Fluid Power Equipment Maintenance – Levels 1 and 2;
- Food Preparation – Level 1;
- Plumbing – Level 1;
- Garment Production – Level 1;

- Graphic Design / Desktop Publishing – Levels 1 and 2;
- Grow Box Production – Level 1;
- Heavy Machinery Operations – Levels 1 and 2;
- Home Furnishings – Levels 1 and 2;
- Home Furnishings – Levels 1 and 2;
- Live Sound Engineering – Levels 1 and 2;
- Pastry (Bread, Cakes and Pastries) – Level 1;
- Television and Video Production – Level 1; and
- Woodworking and Furniture Design – Level 1.

Like the NESC programmes, the YTEPP courses can be used for business ventures for SMEs. In this regard, T&T can act as a model for Guyana and Suriname as it reveals the type of technical vocational programmes that should be developed to complement the hydrocarbon industry.

Notably, while these technical vocational skill sets provide significant scope for employment creation, several individuals residing in T&T, Guyana, and Suriname do not have the financial capital to start a business. Furthermore, they do not have access to a good market location, they are challenged in finding clients, and they do not have any training in microeconomics to guide them about the management of the cash flow of their business.

6.4 Niche Industries

There is room for entrepreneurs from T&T, Guyana, and Suriname to capture value from niche industries. One niche industry that can be targeted by the countries is the gold jewellry industry.

The gold jewellry industry is a potential industry that can be developed in Guyana and Suriname. Presently, Guyana and Suriname are endowed with gold reserves. The value chain for gold in the countries comprises of three major segments, namely: i) upstream - mineral exploration; ii) midstream - gold dealing and trading; iii) downstream - jewellry making and distribution.

Upstream in the mineral exploration segment of the value chain, there are several artisanal and small scale-miners (ASSM). There was a large-scale mining company in Guyana, Omai, but it exited the industry in 2005. The ASSM often mines without a licence, and practices unsustainable mining measures, resulting in land degradation, deforestation, and mercury pollution in waterways.

The midstream section of the value chain in Guyana includes the sale of unrefined gold to the local authority. The Guyana Gold Board (GGB) is authorized to purchase domestically extracted gold from artisanal miners. The ASSMs are paid a price based on the London Bullion Market daily fixes. The GGB exports through the Royal Canadian Mint, where the gold is sent to be refined and then marketed through the Board's overseas agent, Mitsui and Company Precious Metals Inc. Approximately 99 percent of the officially declared gold is exported (Pasha et al. 2017). The residual remains in the local market are used as the primary inputs for gold jewellry (Thomas 2009; Pasha et al. 2017).

The prices offered by the GGB to the local miners are usually lower than the international price as an allowance is made for impurities in the gold, and deductions are made for the gold royalty and other taxes. As a result, some domestic miners smuggle the gold out of the country to avoid paying taxes and to fetch better prices (Pasha et al. 2017). Approximately one-third of the gold extracted in the country is not reported.

Apart from the smuggling challenge experienced in the upstream segment of the gold value chain, the jewellers in the downstream segment also face several hurdles. The domestic market for locally produced jewellry in Guyana is small. Jewellers sell their finished products to consumers and tourists. While it is logical to look at the international market to export, the local jewellers are faced with several constraints. The main bottlenecks include:

- lack of international contacts;
- lack of market information (e.g. how to export, advanced rulings on trade, target markets, etc.);
- inadequate support services (e.g. shipping, insurance, packaging, the supply of raw materials, etc.);
- weak access to export finance; and
- weak trade facilitation and export promotion (KEA 2015).

The limited domestic market opportunities for jewellers in Guyana can be addressed by the intra-regional trade between Guyana and T&T in the gold industry.

Entrepreneurs in T&T can import gold from the ASSM in Guyana. Once the gold is imported legitimately, the respective export taxes can be paid to the public authorities (GGB) in Guyana. If the gold is exported in an unprocessed form, it can be processed in T&T to produce a variety of gold jewellry. Presently, the GORTT Ministry of Community Development offers a short course in the manufacturing of jewellry. Additionally, the UTT offers an additional programme, a Bachelor of Fine Arts in Fashion Design. Even if the gold is exported as jewellry, it can still be sold to jewellers in T&T.

While this intra-regional trade in gold may sound 'new', multinational private-sector companies practice cross-country industrialization as part of their global value chain strategy to produce products for the world market. Multinational private sector companies' head offices are often located in countries that do not have all the natural resources they need to produce their product. As a result, they set up operations in different countries, and they import raw materials from different countries to attain the required factor inputs to produce their product. Additionally, the final product is often exported to foreign markets to fetch the highest prices and to maximise profits.

Therefore, there is room for T&T, Guyana, and Suriname to unpause the CARICOM Single Market Economy (CSME) and trade the products which are abundant in their countries.

6.5 Export Professional Services

The subsidisation of tertiary education may eventually result in an oversupply of some tertiary education skills in countries. While there may not be sufficient employment opportunities to utilise these skills in each country, they can be useful worldwide. Therefore, it would be rational if these graduates export their services.

Services can be exported through four channels:

- Mode 1: Consumption by foreigners – this includes the provision of services to foreign visitors;
- Mode 2: Cross-border supply – this refers to the situations where the services cross international boundaries, but the service supplier remains in their home country, for example, the provision of services through telecommunications;
- Mode 3: Commercial presence – this is where locals are allowed to establish businesses in foreign countries, thus exporting their services; and
- Mode 4: Movement of natural persons – this is where locals are allowed to emigrate to foreign countries to supply their labour.

CARICOM has signed bilateral preferential trade agreements (PTAs) with

- Colombia (July 24, 1994, and which entered into force on June 1, 1995);
- Costa Rica (signed on March 9, 2004);
- Cuba (signed on July 5, 2000);
- the Dominican Republic (signed on August 22, 1998, and provisionally entered into force in December 2001); and
- Venezuela (signed on October 15, 1992, and entered into force on January 1, 2000).

CARICOM and the Dominican Republic have also negotiated a regional economic partnership agreement with the European Union, the CARIFRORUM-EU EPA. The Commonwealth Caribbean countries, also have nonreciprocal PTAs with Canada, under the Caribbean Canada Trade Agreement (CARIBCAN)[36]. Caribbean countries also benefit from nonreciprocal preferential trade with the United States (US), under the Caribbean Basin Initiative (CBI)[37].

Out of all the aforementioned PTAs, only the CARIFORUM-EU EPA offers the prospects of trade in services. The CRNM (2009) notes

> *"The EU opened 29 sectors to allow professional employees of CARIFORUM firms referred to as "contractual service suppliers" (CSS) to*

---

[36] CARIBCAN was signed in 1986 between the Government of Canada, the CARICOM Member States. As a nonreciprocal PTA, CARIBCAN is not consistent with the World Trade Organisation's (WTO's) principles on non-discrimination. Therefore, Canada requires a WTO Most Favoured Nation (MFN) waiver to grant non-reciprocal preferential treatment to the CARICOM Member States (Deonarine et al. 2016). CARIBCAN was scheduled to expire on December 31, 2013. However, Canada successfully requested a waiver from the WTO to extend CARIBCAN for up to 10 years after its expiration date. Therefore, CARIBCAN will expire in 2023 (BCCI 2018).

[37] The US offered unreciprocated preferential market access to the Caribbean region under the CBI in 1984. The CBI was launched in 1983 through the Caribbean Basin Economic Recovery Act (CBERA). It was later expanded in 2000 through the US-Caribbean Basin Trade Partnership Act (CBTPA) and again by the Trade Act of 2002. CBERA took effect from January 1, 1984 and has no set expiration date. The CBTPA is scheduled to expire on September 30, 2020 (OUSTR 2018). CBI is also inconsistent with the WTO's principle of non-discrimination and MFN. The US successfully obtained a MFN waiver from the WTO to extend the CBI, however, the waiver is scheduled to end by December 31, 2019 (The Daily Observer 2019).

enter the EU to supply services for up to 6 months in a year. This includes new areas such as entertainment, fashion model, chef de cuisine services, which do not need university degrees. Eleven (11) sectors have been opened up to allow self-employed CARIFORUM professionals to enter the EU to supply services for up to 6 months" (CRNM 2009, 7).

Table 6.02 provides an overview of the different categories of people who may provide services to the EU.

Table 6.02: Labour Allowed to Provide Services to the EU

Category of person	Main criteria	Length of stay allowed
Business visitors	Persons responsible for setting up a commercial presence and paid by a source outside of the host territory.	90 days per calendar year
Intra-corporate transfers Managers, and specialists	Persons employed by a company in the sending country at least a year before entry to the host country to work within a partner company there.	Up to 3 years
Graduate trainees	University graduates, employed by a company for at least a year and entering either Party for career development or training in a branch or parent company.	Up to 1 year
Business services sellers	Persons entering to negotiate a sale or an agreement but who receive remuneration from a source outside of a Party and do not make direct sales.	90 days per year
Contractual service suppliers	Professionals with 3 years experience employed by a company in the sending country, which does not have a presence in the other party but has a service contract with a client in the other party.	Up to 6 months per year

Independent professionals	Self-employed professionals with 6 years experience and service contract.	Up to 6 months per year
Short-term visitors for business purpose	Persons that are not selling services can enter either Party to perform a range of activities such as: research and design, marketing research, training, trade fairs and exhibitions, sales, purchasing and tourism	Up to 90 days per year

Source: CRNM (2009)

It is noteworthy that market access does not guarantee market penetration. Therefore, even in the face of preferential market access, it does not guarantee that the people will be able to easily flow (migrate) from the hydrocarbon-rich CARICOM Member States to the target countries to supply their labour.

Since this deficiency has been identified, there is room for the CARIFORUM to negotiate for greater market access, and trade facilitation for the export of services, more specifically, the free movement of natural persons in its future trade agreements.

It is noteworthy that a review of the EPA is supposed to occur every 5 years. The review process could result in the amendment of some of the provisions of the EPA. The review and amendment could be triggered by:

1. Unilateral undertakings.
2. The triggering of review clauses of the EPA could then be implemented by the Trade and Development Committee or the Joint CARIFORUM-EU Council.
3. A bilateral renegotiation of provisions of the EPA.

Since the EPA was signed in the year 2008, a review should have occurred in 2013, and later in 2018. However, the most recent review occurred in 2015 (EC 2015a). Although data limitations have prevented the identification of deficiencies in the trade in services, there is scope for the GORTT to renegotiate, as part of CARIFORUM, for better market access by the movement of natural persons when the next review process is scheduled to occur in 2020.

CARIBCAN expired on December 31st, 2013. However, Canada successfully requested a waiver from the WTO to extend the non-reciprocated preferences to CARICOM for 10 years. The waiver is scheduled to expire in 2023, creating scope for Canada and CARICOM to negotiate a new PTA, which may be grounded in reciprocated preferences to comply with the WTO rules on non-discrimination.

When CARICOM goes to negotiate with Canada and the US in the near future, it should negotiate for preferential treatment in services. More importantly, the CARICOM Member States should negotiate for the liberalisation of services in all 4 modes.

6.6 Summary Insight

The key to sustainable inclusive growth is enabling more people to secure productive employment. This can be done through the promotion of sectors that have the potential to absorb labour. The hydrocarbon-rich CARICOM Member States are fortunate to possess several industries with tremendous potential.

The first industry with the potential is the education sector. The region already has an affinity for developing offshore universities for the training of international students. This niche can be further developed, and encouraged for the exporting of a wider range of educational programmes. This can be beneficial to labour within the region especially if qualified professionals are granted opportunities to offer teaching and lecturing services.

The second industry is the creative industry. The region's music, culture, and festivals are unique. The product differentiation provided distinguishes the CARICOM region from other tourist destinations. There is scope to further leverage the region's creative industries to earn more foreign exchange and capture more income for a wide range of stakeholders.

Third, the region also possesses niche industries. The gold industry is an example of this. While countries such as Guyana and Suriname are endowed with commercial reserves of gold, the size of their domestic market is small. This limitation can be easily addressed by exporting to neighbouring countries. This presents a win to both the exporters and the importers, as revenue can be generated by stakeholders from different stages of the value chain.

The fourth industry is the export of professional services. This is the natural solution to the surplus labour in the countries. Emphasis should be placed by the CARICOM Member States in gaining preferential access in international markets to export services. This can allow for the earning of foreign exchange, and facilitate the transitioning of the labour force from low productive areas into higher productive ventures.

The next chapter reviews the policy recommendations required to generate the appropriate enabling environment for entrepreneurship and employment creation in the hydrocarbon-rich CARICOM Member States.

CHAPTER SEVEN

POLICY RECOMMENDATIONS TO ENCOURAGE ENTREPRENEURSHIP

Several options can be applied by the policy makers in the hydrocarbon-rich CARICOM Member States to address the employment problem. This study recommends: 1) the promotion of entrepreneurship through business incubation; 2) the provision of career guidance to young people from the secondary school level; and 3) the creation of an enabling environment to facilitate e-commerce. The aforementioned policy options are discussed in the following subsections.

7.1 Entrepreneurship and Business Incubation

As previously mentioned, every year thousands of students graduate from tertiary educational programmes. Although windfall hydrocarbon revenues can allow a government to create make-shift work to suppress its country's unemployment rate, this may occur at the expense of productivity. Therefore, it is unrealistic for a government aspiring to build a competitive economy to employ all the people in its country.

While anyone can create a business, several constraints hinder the success of many businesses. Common reasons include bad management by the business owners, negative macroeconomic shocks, poor sales, and a weak enabling environment. Business incubation programmes have been known to increase the probability of success of businesses.[38] Therefore, this study recommends that a business incubation programme should be implemented to encourage entrepreneurship, and increase the probability of success of businesses.

Generally speaking, an incubator is a mechanism that is used to keep premature babies warm and safe in a controlled environment. In the same

---

[38] A business incubator was first used in Batavia, New York in the United States in 1959. Since then, it has been used in several countries (Obaji et al. 2015).

vein business incubation is a programme targeted at keeping infant firms safe through an array of support services, until they are strong and sufficiently matured to move out of the incubator and thrive on their own (Obaji et al. 2015).

Business incubators are designed to generate the appropriate enabling environment for businesses, especially SMEs, by helping reduce the cost of launching the business, increase the confidence and capacity of the entrepreneur, link the entrepreneur to the resources required to produce goods and services, and connect the entrepreneur with access to markets to get sales. Entrepreneurs should stay in the incubators as long as it takes to reach specific milestones, often measured in terms of revenue, profitability, and productive capacity (Khalil and Olafsen 2010).

An effective coupling of innovation and entrepreneurship requires what can be described as an ecosystem with active linkages between various stakeholders such as academics, financial institutions, policymakers, and entrepreneurs. If the aforementioned network between the stakeholders is weak or non-existent, the entire ecosystem is not as effective at enabling innovative entrepreneurship.

Business incubators have a unique position in this ecosystem. They interact with all the stakeholders in the ecosystem, and try to build relationships necessary to support the entrepreneurs. The business incubators are also in the position to observe all the challenges the entrepreneurs face, which in turn could be forwarded to the policy makers to better inform the entrepreneurship and people-centred industrial policy. An information loop can be developed within the ecosystem which can be used to identify opportunities for other actors within the network. For example, financial institutions can learn about the risks of various business ventures, removing the asymmetric information barrier in loans. Universities can capitalise on research opportunities as lecturers and post-graduate students may study a wide range of the problems the SMEs face, which may produce useful recommendations for industries.

It is noteworthy that business incubation is selective, in the sense that it selects growth-oriented entrepreneurs and tries to help them develop and become successful. However, it is distasteful to "leave behind" entrepreneurs that do not have a sense of direction. In this regard, this study recommends that a direction-oriented business incubation programme should be developed. Alternatively expressed, the business incubation programme should help guide SMEs in specific business ventures. For example, the business incubation can target specific sectors that the countries have competence in, such as:

- creative industries;
- technical vocational services; and
- niche industries.

The business incubation programme should have 3 components: i) educational training; ii) business finance; iii) business mentorship; and iv) monitoring and evaluation.

Phase I – Educational Training

In the first phase of the business incubation programme, the individual that enrolled should undergo educational training. Presently, people in the CARICOM Member States have a culture where they pursue an education to go to work for someone else after graduation. The business incubation programme seeks to break that culture, by providing people with education and training which can be used to generate employment and income-earning opportunities for themselves.

To achieve this, the individuals enrolled in the business incubation programme should be trained in both business (and economics), as well as at least one technical vocational area. This is consistent with the policy direction of Nigeria, Malaysia, and Singapore. In the business and economics training, the individuals should be thought:

- how to keep records;
- how to develop a business plan;
- how to understand cash flows;
- how to pay their taxes and file tax returns;
- costing, pricing, and tendering for contracts;
- about micro economic principles such as marginal, average, and total costs and revenue; and
- about demand, supply, elasticity, profit maximisation, and the theory of the firm.

The technical vocational areas include:

- welding;
- air conditioning and refrigeration – installation and maintenance;
- carpentry, wood working, and furniture design;

- plumbing;
- derrick man;
- electrical installation – domestic, industrial, and commercial;
- heavy equipment operation;
- industrial mechanical maintenance;
- computer networking;
- media production (music, video, photography, graphic design);
- automotive repair and maintenance;
- drilling rig operations;
- cosmetology and nail design;
- agro-processing; and
- food preparation.

T&T has a head start as it has several technical-vocational institutions. While Guyana and Suriname are waiting for sufficient revenue to develop their educational potential, it would be rational for the countries to send their students to T&T for training. This move will also help the CSME function as a mechanism that facilitates the development of the region.

Individuals that have already obtained the technical-vocational skills from one of the existing institutions may proceed to pursue the business/ economics training before proceeding to phase two of the business incubation programme. Individuals that have both the technical vocational training, as well as the business/ economics training may proceed to phase two.

Phase II – Business Finance

In the second phase of the business incubation programme, the individual may be encouraged to form a business. The business may be a sole trader, partnership, or limited liability company. After formally registering the business with the Ministry of Legal Affairs in the respective country, and obtaining the relevant number to pay taxes, the business owner may then seek financing. If the business owners have sufficient equity, they may proceed to phase three of the incubation programme. If they have insufficient finance, the business incubation programme may directly provide loan financing for the entrepreneurs.

T&T enjoyed many years of windfall hydrocarbon revenue, and thus has developed strength in financing programmes. They include:

i. The Ministry of the Social Development and Family Services (MSDFS), implements the Micro-Enterprise and Training Grant (METG) program which provides a grant up to a maximum of $5,000.00 paid directly to suppliers of the goods or services, to help individuals start a small business.
ii. The Ministry of Labour and Small and Micro Enterprise Development (MLSMED), formerly implemented the National Integrated Business Incubation System (IBIS) which provided 3 categories of loans: i) less than TT $100,000; ii) between TT $100,000 to TT $250,000; and iii) between TT$250,000 and TT $500,000 (NEDCO 2015). While the IBIS programme was a good idea, it was not well promoted, and it lacked a technical training component to equip people with labour-intensive skills to pursue business activities.
iii. The National Entrepreneurship Development Company Limited (NEDCO) provides business loans up to TT$250,000 for first-time borrowers, and up to TT$500,000 for second-time borrowers. NEDCO also has an Entrepreneurial Training Institute and Incubation Centre (ETIIC), which provides business training to SMEs seeking and in receipt of loans.
iv. The Development Finance Limited (DFL) provides loan financing which can enhance, improve, expand or increase the business opportunity for any business owner. DFL has no loan ceiling and can assess a project or loan application on its merit. Moreover, DFL can provide financing for plant and equipment needs, raw materials, refurbishment, information technology upgrades, vehicle acquisition, agro-processing, construction and infrastructure works, manufacturing, contracts, and international trade.
v. The Business Development Unit (BDU) of the Division of Finance and Enterprise Development in Tobago provides loans to start-ups and existing businesses in Tobago. Similar to other state-funded loan programs, the BDU provides training to SMEs in financial management, and business management.
vi. The Youth Business Trinidad and Tobago (YBTT) provides loans to young people in T&T, up to a maximum of TT$30,000. While the YBTT will fund many business enterprises, certain business ventures (such as bars, gambling enterprises, internet cafés, DVD stores, mini-marts, and motor vehicles) lie outside of its mandate.
vii. The Agriculture Development Bank provides financing for stakeholders involved in agriculture, and fishing in T&T. The institution distributes loans for business start-ups, the purchase of

tools and equipment, material, and other inputs for farming and fishing.

viii. Several credit unions in T&T provide loans to individuals. As previously mentioned, credit unions tend to provide loans with lower interest rates, and are more lenient about loan repayment than banks.

ix. The Venture Capital Incentive Program (VCIP) was introduced to increase the accessibility of financial capital for small business owners in T&T. The program facilitates venture capital, and enables large firms to provide finance to SMEs which they believe have high growth potential in exchange for equity.

x. The Ministry of Trade and Industry offers the Grant Fund Facility which provides grant financing to SMEs to purchase capital equipment and inputs geared towards export. The grant covers 8 sectors: financial; maritime; aviation; fish and fish processing; software design and applications; creative industries; agriculture and agro-processing; and manufacturing subsectors.

xi. ExporTT administers the Research and Development Facility (RDF), which provides grant financing to SMEs to 1) manufacturing and service firms to develop innovative/exportable products, processes, systems, and services; 2) help SMEs obtain intellectual properties rights; 3) foster easier modification of products to satisfy export markets; and 4) mobilise resources to assist in the commercialisation of their product.

xii. The Export-Import Bank of Trinidad and Tobago (EXIMBANK) is the only financial institution in T&T whose mandate is to provide credit to businesses to facilitate and encourage their exports. Although the EXIMBANK is owned by the Government of the Republic of Trinidad and Tobago (GORTT), it raises funds on the financial market, which it uses to generate loans to businesses already engaging in the export of goods. It is noteworthy that the EXIMBANK's stakeholders are not small enterprises since a business must develop to a point where it can produce a large output, and meet the demands of at least 1 importer in an international market, to effectively participate in international trade.

Despite these financing initiatives, many people in T&T continue to look towards the government for jobs, rather than focusing on innovation and developing new opportunities. One of the reasons for this failure is the disjointed connection between finance, the education and training to produce goods and services, and information about market opportunities.

Indeed, the business incubation programme would need to connect all three avenues to be effective.

The business incubation programme can pool new finance to fund the business loans for entrepreneurs. However, to prevent the duplication of efforts, and to avoid the trouble of trying to find new finance, the government could bring all of its SME financing options under the proposed business incubation programme. At the inception, the SMEs could be allowed to access a small loan ranging with an upper limit of $50,000. However, when they repay the loan, they could qualify for a larger loan to upgrade their productive capacity.

Phase III – Business Mentorship

In the third phase, a mentor or business incubator could be allocated to each business. The mentor would be required to assess the needs of the business, and assign a programme to strengthen and accelerate the business. The business mentor should be proactive, in helping the entrepreneur:

- identify their target market;
- source potential clients for their goods or service;
- identify where they could source raw materials necessary for production;
- identify possible locations for the sale of goods and services;
- verify the financial statements, and financial management practices;
- evaluate the business readiness to export to different markets; and
- record the challenges encountered in the business.

It is noteworthy that several business mentorship programmes were attempted in T&T. For instance, NEDCO formerly provided business mentorship through the Entrepreneurial Training Institute and Incubation Centre. The programme sought to build the capacity of entrepreneurs in T&T so that they could:

- develop realistic and practical business ideas;
- create a business plan;
- pinpoint the major issues with starting a business;
- understand the importance of business planning; and
- consider the relevant important factors when starting a business in Trinidad and Tobago.

NEDCO also provided mentorship to individuals through the IBIS programme. IBIS was composed of 2 types of incubators, a Community-Based Business Incubator (CBBI), and a Commercial Business Incubators (CBI). The CBBI sought to leverage business activities based on the resources of the target community. They targeted the following communities: Chaguanas, Couva, Diego Martin, Laventille, Barataria/ San Juan, Point Fortin, and Sande Grande (Singh 2013).

In comparison, the CBI was geared towards the development of businesses for national economic transformation (NEDCO 2015). The CBBI option was more common than the CBI, since it applied to SMEs.

The CBBI incubator had 6 stages. The first was candidate selection, then followed by an orientation, then by a skills development stage. The last 3 stages included post-incubation, business incubation, then finally business proposition (NEDCO 2015).

In December 2019, the NEDCO launched the Business Accelerator, which is a programme that seeks to encourage the growth in the number of entrepreneurship ventures in T&T. The Business Accelerator is scheduled to begin from January 2020, and will initially be run in partnership with the tertiary education institutions operating within T&T. Its target market is tertiary students that have an existing business, and those that are interested in starting a new business (Trinidad and Tobago Newsday 2019). As the initiative seeks to marry business mentoring with business finance, no prior experience is needed. All that is required is an idea, and the objective of the programme is to help bring the idea to a successful realisation/ reality.

In 2014, the University of Trinidad and Tobago launched the uSTART programme, the first university-originated business incubator in T&T (GORTT 2014). uSTART business incubator targets the following sectors:

- digital/animation;
- fashion;
- agro-processing; and
- sound recording.

In 2013, UWI's Arthur Lok Jack Graduate School of Business (ALJGSB) launched the Business Booster Commercial Incubator programme (Biz-Booster), which targeted entrepreneurs in Tobago. The programme provided business mentorship for the start-ups in Tobago.

Phase IV – Monitoring and Evaluation

In the fourth phase, the mentor could be required to report the performance of the business to the relevant ministry. The ministry can use several monitoring and evaluation officers to assess the challenges, and identify potential gaps in the business incubation framework. This in turn can be analysed by the policy officers in the ministry, and help inform amendments to the business incubation framework over time.

7.2 Career Guidance and Entrepreneurship Education

In the hydrocarbon-rich CARICOM Member States, entrepreneurship as a career option is often a marginalised choice because the general curricula of education emphasises academics. Moreover, people are socialised to obtain qualifications to go and work as an employee for an employer.

Although the education system in the CARICOM Member States was influenced by the country's colonial heritage, the European Commission (EC) has recognised the flaw in its old education system and how it contributes to high youth unemployment. Subsequently, entrepreneurship is prominent on the agenda of the European Commission. In its 2012 report on rethinking its education strategy, it asserts

> *"all young people should benefit from entrepreneurship education, including at least one practical entrepreneurial experience before leaving compulsory education"* (EC 2015b, 17).[39]

Certainly, the CARICOM Member States can benefit if there is a shift in thinking, and new enterprises are viewed as the most important source of employment and income-earning opportunities rather than employment with the government. Furthermore, given the vulnerabilities in the countries' hydrocarbon sector, the country could achieve sustained inclusive economic growth by producing highly versatile people whose innovation and entrepreneurial activities contribute to the economy.

Entrepreneurship education can be implemented in multiple ways. The main types are:

- National strategies – this is where countries draft policies and strategies which formulate specific goals and objectives related to entrepreneurship education.

[39] The EC 2020 development strategy aspires to achieve the aforementioned objective.

- Courses and classes – this is where educational institutions introduce entrepreneurship education in the form of individual courses and classes. This can be implemented at the pre-university level, university level, and technical vocational level.
- Institutional changes – this is where there is a real change in the education system and the focus is on producing graduates that will become entrepreneurs rather than seek to become an employee. The focus is to provide students with useful skills which can give them opportunities to earn their income rather than relying on the wage from an employer. This calls for the building of an effective relationship between industries, and educational institutions, so that the schools can be informed about the needs of the industries, and update their curriculum accordingly. Teachers would be required to update their skills through regular training, and young people would have to be trained in workplaces that can utilise their skills rather than be allocated to "make shift work" programmes where they will be paid to do nothing.

Ideally, the "institutional change" option should be implemented. However, this would be difficult given that the countries have spent decades in the old colonial educational system. Furthermore, there needs to be a buy-in by all stakeholders, namely the educational institutions (at the primary, secondary, technical vocational, and tertiary level), the employers, the ministries implementing the policy, and most importantly, the people.

This institutional change is a shift that a government will not be able to implement overnight. Instead, it would have to be done over several years. This could be implemented in 3 phases.

In the first phase, to produce tangible results, the government could consider rolling out an entrepreneurship education programme that complements the proposed business incubation programme.

The people enrolled in the business incubation programme could be taught the entrepreneurship opportunities which can arise from different skill sets. As part of the incubation programme, the people can be taught how to become an entrepreneur. For example, assume a person was trained in electrical installation. They can be taught how to import the required material to set up a store to sell electrical supplies. They could also be taught how to write proposals, and bid for contracts to do electrical installation work for their target market. The success of young people in business could be used as case studies to guide more people in the future.

In the second phase, the entrepreneurship education programme could be expanded to target secondary schools, technical vocational schools, and tertiary education institutions. In this phase, workshops should be conducted to educate people about the business opportunities. To make the entrepreneurship education programme more streamlined, the workshops can target sectors identified in Chapter Six, namely, creative industries, technical vocational industries, and niche industries.

During the workshops, the students should be taught what are the steps required to develop certain businesses. For example, if a student aspires to open a marine bunkering firm, they should be informed about what is required to establish the business venture. Since students may not be able to implement these businesses in their teenage years, but may be willing to do so in their adult years, the students should be given an electronic copy of this information. Additionally, the ministries implementing these workshops should save these workshop exercises in a website, which is accessible to the entire public.

In the third phase, there could be a reform of the educational system. Rather than base the secondary school curriculum solely based on academics, there could be a greater incorporation of technical vocational education from the secondary school level. Students could be given the option to subjects in technical vocational areas, for example, auto mechanics, electronics, computer networking, etc., which they will be assessed upon at the CXC or CSEC exams. It is noteworthy that the CXC and CSEC examinations are Caribbean examinations, not national examinations. Subsequently, there will need to be a discussion at the CARICOM level to instigate this regional change in education.

In the third phase, there should also be a shift in the education system towards providing training in areas that are useful rather than pure academics. This would require action by the tertiary educational institutions to offer programmes which may equip people with skills that can be capitalised upon in business ventures. As the CARICOM Member States are democracies, this shift should be voluntary rather than forced. The governments could use moral suasion to persuade the educational institutions to offer the desired training programmes.

Ideally, the government funding should be targeted at the programmes which can help the governments achieve their development needs. To avoid public political criticism, perhaps the ideal solution may be to offer enhanced incentives for academic areas that are aligned with the government's development objectives, and to leave the existing tertiary education subsidisation in the other areas untouched.

Another approach would be for the government to try to convince young people to pursue career paths in areas identified as the country's development needs. In this regard, the workshop identified in Phase 2 could be used to achieve this objective.

7.3 E-commerce

Entrepreneurship can also be facilitated by electronic commerce (e-commerce). E-commerce, which refers to any form of business transaction in which the parties interact electronically rather than by physical contact, can be a useful tool in creating an enabling environment for entrepreneurship.

E-commerce provides several advantages.

- The first is it performs as a marketing tool and helps connect buyers with sellers. This can improve marketing productivity, and increase the range of customers for suppliers. This is very advantageous as it allows suppliers to connect with customers in different countries, providing an avenue for the suppliers to participate in international trade.
- The second is it reduces the costs of transactions. It allows buyers to avoid multiple intermediaries in their search for information about suppliers, products, and prices. For suppliers, allows for the automation of transactions, which increases efficiency, and helps reduce labour costs.
- Third, it improves price transparency. It allows for the pooling of price information from several sellers which creates opportunities for the customers to purchase goods and services at the lowest prices.
- Fourth, as it connects buyers with sellers, suppliers do not have to operate a physical store in an accessible location to get sales. This allows small-scale suppliers to save on rent.

There are four permutations of e-commerce models.

i) Business to Business (B2B) where electronic transactions occur between businesses;
ii) Business to Customer (B2C) where electronic transactions occur between businesses and consumers;

iii) Customer to Business (C2B) which is similar to the B2C arrangement, however, in this model reverse pricing occurs and the customer determines the prices of the good or services in the transaction; and
iv) Customer to Customer (C2C) which refers to transactions between customers in an auction type model (Patel and Soni 2013).

SMEs can use e-commerce through the B2C model. They can use the internet to market and sell their goods and services to a wide range of customers both domestically and internationally.

For any entrepreneur to sell their goods or services through the internet, they must use an interface available on a website. The entrepreneur has three options in which they can do this. They can: i) build their website to sell their goods and/or services; ii) use a social media platform; and iii) utilise an e-commerce platform.

While the first option may be open to any business, in practice, not every entrepreneur can develop their website with a secure e-commerce interface. SMEs that lack programming skills can easily use a what-you-see-is-what-you-get (WYSIWYG) editor to build their website. However, a secure system within the website is required to enable electronic transactions between parties. This can only be implemented by personnel with extensive knowledge about programming and encryption, skills that would be obtained from a Computer Science degree. Many SMEs do not have these skills, and do not have the financial capital to purchase these skills from the appropriate personnel. Therefore, the first option is likely to be used only by the larger-scale entrepreneurs that have the financial resources to hire the technical personnel to develop and continuously maintain their e-commerce website.

The second option is practical and is very often used by both large-scale and small-scale entrepreneurs. Many social media platforms, such as Facebook, and Twitter, are used to advertise goods and services. However, these social media platforms do not facilitate payments. Entrepreneurs must resort to alternative means, such as the use of wire transfers through banks, or innovative payment platforms like PayPal or WiPay, to enable online payments.

The third option is highly attractive. An e-commerce platform allows sellers to advertise their goods and services, and sell their offerings to different buyers. What is even more advantageous is the sellers do not need any knowledge about website design and computer security to access the e-commerce platform. They are only required to register their business activities with the e-commerce platform, and link their bank accounts to sell their offerings through the platform.

There are several e-commerce platforms available in developed countries. Websites such as Amazon, and Ebay, are examples of two popular e-commerce platforms that service the countries in North America. Unfortunately, there is a shortage of public e-commerce platforms to connect buyers and sellers in the CARICOM Member States.

The Inter-American Development Bank (IDB) recognised the deficiency in e-commerce in the Latin America and Caribbean (LAC) region, and responded by forming the website - Connect Americas, the first social network for businesses in the LAC region. Connect Americas aspires to act as a platform to bridge the suppliers, especially SMEs, with buyers in the LAC region. In 2018, Connect Americas reported that it had a total of 130,000 registered companies, of which 144 were in T&T (Charles 2019b).

While Connect Americas is a commendable step in the right direction, many consumers in T&T are not aware of the website. Furthermore, the website is not as user-friendly for navigation to identify the products being offered as Amazon or Ebay, and the website does not facilitate online payments.

This study recommends that the governments of the hydrocarbon-rich CARICOM Member States take a step forward by creating an e-commerce platform for the country's SMEs. The e-commerce platform should be rolled out as part of a programme to promote entrepreneurship.

> *"The e-commerce platform should:*
> - *contain a system for vendors and consumers to register and create an account at any point in time for free;*
> - *allow the suppliers to advertise their goods and/or service to a wide pool of buyers;*
> - *allow consumers to compare the prices of different vendors;*
> - *allow anyone visiting the website to easily see the products available for sale without having to register on the website;*
> - *allow vendors and consumers to link a bank account or credit card account to their personal account on the e-commerce platform in order to facilitate electronic transactions;*
> - *allow electronic transactions between venders and consumers;*
> - *allow all transactions to be conducted in one common currency, perhaps the United States dollar (USD);*

- *allow the domestic currency to be converted to USD to facilitate transactions;*
- *allow consumers and vendors to link their account on the e-commerce platform to their PayPal account;*
- *allow for the sale of small quantities as well as large quantities of items;*
- *allow for shipping to any legitimate address in Caribbean countries to enable cross-border trade;*
- *allow consumers to track and trace the delivery of their goods;*
- *contain a secure system that is resistant to computer hacks and external internet-based threats;*
- *contain a consumer protection policy, which includes:*
    - *a refund policy if the item delivered is not in the condition that was advertised;*
    - *a refund policy if the consumer did not receive the item, and the vendor cannot produce evidence that the item was posted;*
    - *a warrantee policy;*
    - *a policy which prohibits vendors from transmitting the personal information of consumers to third parties without the consumer's consent.*
- *contain provisions for the consumer to cancel orders and receive a full reimbursement of their funds if they cancel the order before the product has been posted;*
- *contain a framework for consumers to resolve their disputes with vendors;*
- *contain a framework for consumers to evaluate vendors and the products purchased;*
- *contain a framework to protect vendors by the preventing of orders going through to the vendor without the consumer making full payment for the goods;*
- *contain a framework to assess the credibility of customers, and remove customers that develop a reputation for cancelling payments after orders have gone through to the vendor; and*
- *be very user friendly so that anyone would be able to use the platform without any special training"* (Charles 2019b, 264-266).

To prevent the low popularity problem (experienced by Connect Americas) from occurring with the proposed e-commerce platform, the governments could encourage their current SMEs registered with their public authorities (such as the Ministry of Trade and Industry, or the Ministry of Labour) to sign up for the e-commerce services. Entrepreneurs in the proposed business incubation programme could be encouraged to sign up with the e-commerce platform. Furthermore, the e-commerce platform could also be advertised by the government in trade conferences, in the proposed entrepreneurship education campaign, as well as through traditional advertising mechanisms (television, radio, and newspapers).

It is noteworthy that an efficient postal delivery service is required to enable e-commerce activities. The national postal couriers in T&T, Guyana, and Suriname are responsible for fulfilling respective countries' Universal Service Obligation (USO).[40] However, the delivery of the USO is not profitable to national postal couriers. This, as well as competition from several private sector postal operators that do not have a USO, places financial strain on the national postal courier. [41] The profitability challenge, as well as operational inefficiencies, prevents the national postal couriers from operating "day plus one" delivery.

The operational deficiencies of the national postal couriers should be addressed to improve their delivery time. Once this is done and they achieve efficiency levels comparable to the private sector postal operators, they can easily earn additional revenue from parcel trade as goods are traded through e-commerce.

7.4 Summary Insight

There are technical vocational schools in T&T, and financing programmes, yet there is a weak thrust by the graduate population towards entrepreneurship. Action is needed to change the culture from one where almost all graduates aspire to work for someone to one where the graduates move towards harnessing their productive potential through entrepreneurship.

[40] Members of the Universal Postal Union (UPU) agreed that postal services should be available to all areas of countries. This gave rise to the USO mandate which requires national postal companies must provide postal services to all citizens and areas in the country regardless of whether or not it is economical to do so. This USO mandate makes postal services a merit good. Since the provision of postal services are not economically feasible to several locations, governments typically subsidise the USO aspect of their national postal companies.

[41] The private postal companies do not have a USO mandate. Thus, they operate only profitable postal services. The USO forces the national postal couriers to continue to provide postal services on unprofitable routes. Furthermore, the affordability requirement of the USO prevents the governments from raising the national postal couriers' tariffs to high rates.

There is a need to connect technical training with finance, and mentorship. This can be done through business incubation. Business incubation should be implemented in all the hydrocarbon-rich CARICOM Member States.

The second major recommendation of this study is the provision of career guidance to students. Career guidance will be essential in helping channel students towards areas that match the development needs and employment creation opportunities of countries. Additionally, this will be valuable in preventing structural unemployment where there is a mismatch between the skills of the graduate and the employment opportunities available.

The third majour recommendation of this study is the development of e-commerce in the region. This should be promoted as it can enable the Caribbean's SMEs to participate in intra-regional trade. Moreover, e-commerce offers considerable opportunities for SMEs to expand their customer base, generate sustainable incomes, and realise the gains from trade.

The next chapter concludes this study.

CHAPTER EIGHT

GENERAL CONCLUSION

Several developing countries face a common labour problem. There is an excess supply of labour and the governments' desire to find an approximate mix of policies to create employment opportunities for their people.

The Lewis Industrialization by Invitation Model advocates that a developing country should try to attract foreign investors to stimulate economic activity and in turn development. The model assumes the commerce generated by the foreign investors would create opportunities for employment for the local labour force. While a lot of Lewis statements do hold merit, multinational companies only shift their operations to different countries as part of their global value chain strategy to give them an advantage. Thus, foreign investors are more interested in making profits rather than stimulating the economic development of developing countries. Hence the reason why several multinationals are quick to leave developing countries when those operations are not as profitable as before.

Over the years, the GORTT has deployed the Industrialisation by Invitation Model. This allowed the government to expand the industrial base of the energy sector. Energy revenues have also allowed the GORTT to fund public expenditure on various public and merit goods, amongst which the most commendable is the expenditure on education through the GATE programme.

Although it would be advantageous to T&T if the economy can diversify its revenue base, in realistic terms, the country is likely to remain highly dependent upon its energy sector both in the present and the near future. The energy sector is currently under threat from weak domestic production. More specifically, the persistence of the natural gas shortage threatens to undermine the energy sector, as several multinational companies (Mittal Steel, Yara, and Titan) have exited the country. When these companies leave, the workers are left behind and are forced to deal with the harsh reality of retrenchment and unemployment.

Guyana and Suriname are both implementing the Industrialization by Invitation Model. This is evidenced by their inviting of foreign hydrocarbon companies to engage in exploration and production activities in their deep water offshore blocks. Fortunately, both Guyana and Suriname are far away from peak oil and gas, so declining hydrocarbon production is highly unlikely in the near future.

Retrenched workers, as well as new tertiary graduates, are among those without jobs in T&T. Guyana's and Suriname's labour problem is more structural as it would take time to train people to develop the skills that are in demand. Governments may be tempted to provide "make shift work" programmes, but this will comprise productivity, and increase public expenditure. Certainly, no government that is aspiring to build a nation that can competitively compete in liberalised international trade can hire all of the people in its country.

The next logical option is to look towards the private sector for employment creation. However, the private sector is focused on making profits rather than considering the potential public benefits that can be derived from employment, it is often reluctant to employ more labour than it needs. Moreover, the private sector is often hesitant in hiring young workers that may not have the required competence to work.

Indeed, the highlighted concerns are all deficiencies in the current labour market system in the hydrocarbon-rich CARICOM Member State. There is a need for policy action by the governments to correct these deficiencies.

One answer to T&T, Guyana, and Suriname's labour problem may be to fix the inefficiencies in the service commissions. In fact, there were several attempts by the GORTT to reform the public service (see Table 4.03).

Service commission reform and public sector reform in each of the CARICOM Member States is a difficult task since the service commissions are all included in the constitution of the countries. A political administration could only reform the service commissions by amending the constitution. This in turn cannot be done unless a government gains a special majority of three-fourths of all the members of the House of Representatives, and two-thirds of all the members of the Senate. Even if a political administration wins the required amount of seats in the general election to grant it the power to take special majority votes in the House of Representatives, it will not have a special majority in the Senate. Therefore, it would need the support of independent senators and/ or opposition senators to gain the special majority vote. Given the general difficulty of the government to gain the support of the opposition (regardless of which administration that is in power), the government is unlikely to attain the special majority vote in the Senate. Therefore, service commission reform through the amendment of the constitution in the hydrocarbon-rich CARICOM Member States is unlikely in the near future.

The most likely scenario would be the continuation of the dual-employment system in the public service (here public service refers to all the government jobs), where permanent workers are hired through the service commissions and non-permanent workers are hired with fixed-term contracts. Under this system, contract workers are likely to be more vulnerable than permanent workers since the present industrial relations system in the respective countries has no rules that mandates employers to hire workers and renew contracts based on merit. While it is impossible for any law to regulate for every possible scenario, the present industrial relations system leaves the discretion in the hands of the employers to grant contracts.

Generally, the industrial relations framework could be enhanced to improve the social protection of workers in the countries. Moreover, there is room for the amendment of the Industrial Relations Acts, and the other labour laws in T&T, Guyana, and Suriname to reflect and address the issues faced in these modern times.

The study argues that the best response to the employment and job creation problem in T&T, Guyana, and Suriname is to stimulate entrepreneurship. Entrepreneurship is an attractive option as it can create sustainable employment, and provide sustainable income for people. It can also reduce the dependence on the government of the respective countries for employment. Additionally, as entrepreneurs upgrade in capacity, they can export their goods and services, which in turn helps earn foreign exchange for each country.

It is noteworthy that hydrocarbon-rich CARICOM Member States' present education and employment culture does not promote entrepreneurship as a first choice. People are socialised to pursue an education, then to seek to earn income from working for an employer in a job. Furthermore, academic education is promoted over technical vocational education.

This current education-employment culture is flawed. Firstly, the academic education system often encourages a mismatch between education and the requirements for jobs. People obtain knowledge and skills in areas which may not be demanded by the labour market. In an alternate scenario, the academic education system also causes people to obtain knowledge and skills in areas where there are very limited opportunities in the countries. Consequently, the education system often produces graduates that lack the skills to perform jobs, and thus have to be retrained to work.

This mismatch between education and the requirements for jobs splits into 2 additional problems. The first is where employers demand that people have a given number of years' experience, as the graduates need to learn the job to work. The second is where there is an excess supply of skilled workers. The governments have attempted to address the work experience problem with its various training programmes, but its administration of these programmes have been inefficient. Additionally, the overall job training system is highly fragmented and disjointed.

Despite the administrative difficulties, there is room to correct this excess supply of skilled labour problem. This problem could be tackled by the exporting of professional services. The CARICOM Member States have signed trade agreements with many countries (such as Colombia, Costa Rica, Cuba, Dominican Republic, Venezuela, the European Union, the United States, and Canada). However, these trade agreements are more focused on the trade of goods. Effort should be taken by the Member States to negotiate with various international partners for preferential market access to export services. Moreover, effort should be placed to negotiate preferential market access especially from the view of SMEs.

The government, as the leader of the people in the country, should lead its people in the correct career direction. It should implement career guidance programmes where people can be informed from a young age what is the end result of educational training. From this career guidance, two scenarios are desirable. The first is where people pursue education and training in areas where there is scope for employment in each country. Alternatively expressed, people should be encouraged to pursue training in areas which can support labour-intensive industries in T&T, Guyana, and Suriname respectively. Specific sectors such as the creative industry, the hydrocarbon industry, and niche industries, have been identified as excellent industries for employment creation in the hydrocarbon-rich CARICOM Member States. Indeed, technical vocational skills, and engineering skills would emerge as very useful skills in these labour-intensive industries.

The second desirable outcome is where people pursue education and training in areas which provide them with an opportunity to open their own business. Again technical vocational skills would be very useful since there is a multitude of opportunities to commercialise these skills. For instance, there is a real demand for competent mechanics, electricians, surveyors, civil engineers, etc. in the hydrocarbon-rich CARICOM Member States. People with these skills do not need a formal job as they can sell their services to the general public, as well as private sector organisations.

The government of the respective countries should focus its employment creation efforts on encouraging their citizens to become entrepreneurs. It is noteworthy that many citizens of the CARICOM Member States are faced with obstacles that prevent them from becoming successful entrepreneurs on their own. However, this can be corrected by policy action by the respective governments. More specifically, a comprehensive holistic business incubation programme could be implemented to create the right enabling environment to stimulate entrepreneurship.

T&T, as the first to enter the hydrocarbon industry, has attempted several entrepreneurship programmes in the past. They include NEDCO's Community-Based Business Incubator, NEDCO's Business Accelerator, Arthur Lok Jack's Biz-Booster, and UTT's uSTART. However, what distinguishes the proposed business incubation programme from all the rest is the proposal to integrate business mentoring, with educational training, start-up financing, and e-commerce.

The right skills, business knowledge, finance, networks, and markets are the key factors required for SMEs to succeed in business. Therefore, the government of the respective countries should use its policy tools to bring these factors together for SMEs. These initiatives are essential in putting the hydrocarbon-rich CARICOM Member States on the path to sustained inclusive economic growth and social prosperity.

REFERENCES

Akinbode, F.O. 2009. "Perspectives on Entrepreneurship and Skills Development for Students/Youths: Criteria for Achievement of Federal Government Seven-Point Agenda." In *Proceedings of the Entrepreneurship Workshop Held at National Universities Commission*. Abuja, Nigeria, NUC.

Allais, Stephanie. 2012. "Will Skills Save Us? Rethinking the Relationships Between Vocational Education, Skills Development Policies, and Social Policy in South Africa." *International Journal of Educational Development* 32 (5): 632-642.

Allard, Alia. 2012. "The Contribution of Small Farms and Commercial Large Farms to the Food Security of Trinidad and Tobago." Master of Arts, DePaul University.

ACP Secretariat. 2003. "The Cotonou Agreement in a Nutshell." Accessed April 5, 2019. https://ecdpm.org/wp-content/uploads/cotonou-nsa-guide-chapter-2.pdf

Babcock, Jessica M., Blake D. Babcock, and Marshall Z. Schwartz. 2013. "Maintaining a Sufficient and Quality Physician Workforce: The Role of For-Profit Medical Schools." *Health Services Insights* 6: 87-98.

Bai, Jushan and Pierre Perron. 1998. "Estimating and Testing Linear Models with Multiple Structural Changes." *Econometrica* 66: 47–78.

Barrow, Robert., and Xavier Sala-I-Martin. 1995. *Economic Growth*. New York, United States: McGraw-Hill.

Bermúdez-Lugo, Omayra. 2002. "The Mineral Industries of French Guiana, Guyana and Suriname." Accessed January 18, 2022. https://s3-us-west-2.amazonaws.com/prd-wret/assets/palladium/production/mineral-pubs/country/2002/gfgynsmyb02.pdf

Belfor, Jummy. 2006. *A Desk Review on Changing Work Arrangements and the Scope of the Employment Relationship in Suriname*. Trinidad and Tobago: ILO Subregional Office for the Caribbean.

Blomqvist, Hans C. 2000. "Development Policies of Singapore: Dynamics of Internationalisation versus Regionalisation." Proceedings of the University of Vaasa Discussion Papers 275, 37. University of Vaasa, Finland.

Boateng, Christina. 2012. "Restructuring Vocational and Technical Education in Ghana: The Role of Leadership Development." *International Journal of Humanities and Social Science* 2 (4): 108-114.

Boopsingh, Trevor. 2004. "Report of the Energy Sub-Committee for Vision 2020." Accessed October 31, 2019. https://www.laohamutuk.org/Oil/LNG/Refs/028TTVision2020SubCommEnergy.pdf

Boopsingh, Trevor M., and Gregory McGuire. 2014. *From Oil to Gas and Beyond: A Review of the Trinidad and Tobago Model and Analysis of Future Challenges*. New York, United States: University Press of America.

Bridglal, Carla. 2017. "UTT's Cash Woes Trouble Garcia." *Trinidad and Tobago Newsday,* November 5. Accessed November 7, 2019. https://newsday.co.tt/2017/11/05/utts-cash-woes-trouble-garcia/

Campbell, Carl C. 1992. *A Short History of Education in Trinidad and Tobago 1834-1986*. Kingston: Ian Randle Publishers.

CARICOM (Caribbean Community). 2016. "CARICOM Declaration of Labour and Industrial Relations Principles." *Caribbean Community Secretariat*. Accessed August 20, 2016. http://archive.caricom.org/jsp/secretariat/legal_instruments/declaration_labour_principles.jsp

CBTT (Central Bank of Trinidad and Tobago). 2021. "Data Centre." Accessed January 26, 2019. https://www.central-bank.org.tt/statistics/data-centre/debt-annual

CBM (Central Bank of Malaysia). 2019. "Annual Report." Accessed January 19, 2022. https://www.bnm.gov.my/documents/20124/2724769/ar2019_en_full.pdf

Charles, Don. 2019a. "Global Value Chain Analysis of the Agriculture Industry in T&T." In *Enhancing and Capturing More Value from the Caribbean Community's Value Chains.* Cambridge, United Kingdom: Cambridge Scholars Publishing.

—. 2019b. "An E-Commerce Platform for Promoting SME Value Chains in Barbados, Jamaica, and Trinidad and Tobago." In *Enhancing and Capturing More Value from the Caribbean Community's Value Chains*. Cambridge, United Kingdom: Cambridge Scholars Publishing.

COHA (Council on Hemispheric Affairs). 2005. "Banana Wars Continue – Chiquita Once Again Tries to Work Its Omnipotent Will, Now Under New Management: Likely Big Losers Will Be CARICOM's Windward Islands." Accessed April 5, 2019. http://www.coha.org/banana-wars-continue-%e2%80%93-chiquita-once-again-tries-to-work-its-omnipotent-will-now-under-new-management-likely-big-losers-will-be-caricom%e2%80%99s-windward-islands/

Commonwealth Secretariat. 2016. "Key Principles of Public Sector Reforms, Case Studies and Frameworks." Accessed November 3, 2019. https://thecommonwealth.org/sites/default/files/news-items/documents/P14763_PSG_PGSU.pdf

Cong, Sen, and Xiaomei Wang. 2012. "A Perspective on Technical and Vocational Education and Training." *Advances in Computer Science and Engineering* 1: 67–75.

Constant, Louay, Shelly Culbertson, Cathleen Stasz, and Georges Vernez. 2014. "Improving Technical Vocational Education and Training in the Kurdistan Region—Iraq." Accessed November 28, 2019. https://www.rand.org/content/dam/rand/pubs/research_reports/RR200/RR277/RAND_RR277.pdf

CRNM (Caribbean Regional Negotiating Machinery). 2009. "Overview of the CARIFORUM-EC Economic Partnership agreement (EPA)." Accessed November 18, 2019. https://www.carib-export.com/login/wp-content/uploads/2010/01/TradeWins%20EPA%20Overview%20Final.pdf

Cunningham, J. Barton, and Joe Lischeron. 1991. "Defining Entrepreneurship." *Journal of Small Business Management* 29: 45 – 61.

Danns, Donna. 1992. "Crisis, Adjustment and Recovery: The Lessons of Recent Experiences from the Guyana Economy for the Anglophone Caribbean." In *XXIV Regional Programme of Monetary Studies Annual Conference*, 26-29 October, 1992, Nassau, Bahamas.

Dowlat-Rostant, Rhondor. 2019. "UTT Faces Registry Dilemma as Staff Are Sent Home." *Trinidad and Tobago Guardian*, September 1. Accessed November 7, 2019. https://www.guardian.co.tt/news/utt-faces-registry-dilemma-as-staff-are-sent-home-6.2.924278.8a5836c2ae

Downes, Andrew. 1998. "An Economic Analysis of Unemployment in Trinidad and Tobago." Working Paper, No. 381, Inter-American Development Bank, Office of the Chief Economist, Washington, DC, United States.

EC (European Commission). 2015a. "Five Year Review of the CARIFORUM-EU Economic Partnership Agreement Joint Working Document." Accessed November 18, 2019. https://trade.ec.europa.eu/doclib/docs/2016/january/tradoc_154165.pdf

—. 2015b. *Entrepreneurship Education: A Road to Success: A Compilation of Evidence On the Impact of Entrepreneurship Education Strategies and Measures*. Luxembourg: Publications Office of the European Union.

ECLAC (Economic Commission for Latin America and the Caribbean). 2021. "The Pandemic Opens an Opportunity to Restructure Education Systems in the Region and Tackle the "Silent Crisis" in that Sector, Said Specialists at Regional Seminar." Accessed January 26, 2022. https://www.cepal.org/en/pressreleases/pandemic-opens-opportunity-restructure-education-systems-region-and-tackle-silent

Foss, Aaron, Bertrand Laurent, Danielle de Garcia, Henry Charles, Mateusz Pucilowski, Nicole Hazel, Rajwantie Sahai, and Sharene McKenzie. 2013. "Eastern and Southern Caribbean Youth Assessment (ESCYA): Final Report." United States Agency for International Development (USAID). Accessed October 14, 2018. https://www.undp.org/content/dam/trinidad_tobago/docs/DemocraticGovernance/Publications/ESCYA%20Final%20Report%20(FINAL%20SUBMISSION)%2031%20Oct.pdf

Gafar, John. 2004. "The Performance of the Labour Market in Guyana." *Canadian Journal of Development Studies* 25 (4): 663-685.

GHRS (Government Human Resource Services Company Limited). 2014. "Annual Report. October 1st 2013 to September 30th 2014." Accessed November 4, 2019. http://parlcloud.ttparliament.org:8081/PapersLaidViewer/TempFiles/GHRS%20ADMIN.%20Report%202013-2014.pdf

Griffith, Clyde, and Vinita Bihariesingh-Raghoenath. 2016. "Petroleum: A New Economic Boost for Suriname." Accessed July 2, 2021. https://www.geoexpro.com/articles/2013/08/petroleum-a-new-economic-boost-for-suriname

González-Velosa, Carolina, David Rosas, and Roberto Flores. 2016. "On-the-Job Training in Latin America and the Caribbean: Recent Evidence." In *Firm Innovation and Productivity in Latin America and the Caribbean*, edited by Matteo Grazzi and Carlo Pietrobelli, 137-166. London, United Kingdom: Palgrave Macmillan.

GORTT (Government of the Republic of Trinidad and Tobago). 2005. "Budget 2006." Accessed June 3, 2015. https://www.finance.gov.tt/wp-content/uploads/2013/11/pub7.pdf

—. 2014. "MTEST, UTT launch uSTART at UTT Caroni Campus." Accessed December 26, 2019. http://news.gov.tt/content/mtest-utt-launch-ustart-utt-caroni-campus#.XgVY1_wpCUk

—. 2017. "The OJT Programme Stays." Accessed November 1, 2019. http://www.news.gov.tt/content/ojt-programme-stays#.Xby5U9UpCUk

GORTT MPAC (Government of the Republic of Trinidad and Tobago, Ministry of Public Administration and Communications). 2017. "Media Release, Country Could No Longer Afford GHRS." Accessed November 4, 2019. http://www.mpac.gov.tt/node/359

GORTT MSDFS (Government of the Republic of Trinidad and Tobago, Ministry of Social Development and Family Services). 2017. "National Social Mitigation Plan 2017-2022." Accessed October 30, 2019. http://www.social.gov.tt/wp-content/uploads/2017/08/NATIONAL-SOCIAL-MITIGATION-PLAN-JULY-2017.pdf

Hanni, Michael. 2019. "Financing of Education and Technical and Vocational Education and Training (TVET) in Latin America and the Caribbean." ECLAC Macroeconomics and Development Series 200: 1-75.

Hart Group. 2017. "Trinidad and Tobago EITI Report October 1st 2015 - September 30th 2016." Accessed October 25, 2019. https://eiti.org/sites/default/files/documents/tteiti-report.pdf

Hosein, Roger, and Martin Franklin. 2010. "Funding Tertiary Level Education in T&T: An Assessment of the Merits of a Graduate Tax." Accessed October 29, 2019. https://s3.amazonaws.com/academia.edu.documents/18491830/final_wigut_proceedings_4_web.pdf?

IDB (Inter-American Development Bank), BSG (Bureau of Statistics Guyana), ILO (International Labour Organisation). 2017. Guyana Labour Force Survey. Accessed December 29, 2021. https://www.ilo.org/surveyLib/index.php/catalog/2426/download/18743

ILO (International Labour Organisation). 2014. "Ratifications for Trinidad and Tobago." *ILO*. Accessed April 13, 2014. http://www.ilo.org/dyn/normlex/en/f?p=1000:11200:0::NO:11200:P11200_COUNTRY_ID:103138.

—. 2015. "World Employment and Social Outlook, The Changing Nature of Jobs." Accessed November 4, 2019. https://www.ilo.org/wcmsp5/groups/public/---dgreports/---dcomm/---publ/documents/publication/wcms_368626.pdf

Ifill, Mellissa. 2002. "Redefining the Role of the Public Sector in Guyana 1988-1992." Accessed January 27, 2022. https://www.landofsixpeoples.com/news022/ns2102411.htm

James, Freddy. 2013. "The School Improvement Policy Context in Trinidad and Tobago, School Effectiveness and School Improvement." *International Journal of Research, Policy and Practice*, DOI:10.1080/09243453.2013.788522

James, Vanus, Sheldon McLean, Hidenobu Tokuda, Machel Pantin, and Don Charles. 2019. "Trinidad and Tobago Trade Policy 2019-2023: Towards Sustainable Economic Growth and Diversification." *Republic of Trinidad and Tobago Ministry of Trade and United Nations ECLAC.*

Johansen, Søren. 1995. *Likelihood-based Inference in Cointegrated Vector Autoregressive Models*. Oxford, United Kingdom: Oxford University Press.

Jones, Peter. 2003. "The Caribbean Community (CARICOM): Origins, Achievements, The Future." Information Booklet Series II, Economic Development Institute.

Joseph, Oshi, and Matthias O. Nkuda. 2021. "Drivers and Inhibitors of Entrepreneurial Growth: The Nigeria's Situation." *Scholarly Journal of Business Administration* 10 (1): 1-9.

Jules, Didacus. 2008. "Rethinking Education for the Caribbean: A Radical Approach." *Comparative Education* 44 (2): 203–214.

Khalil, Mohsen A., and Ellen Olafsen. 2010. "Enabling innovative entrepreneurship through business incubation." In *The Innovation for Development Report 2009–2010*, edited by Mohsen A. Khalil and Ellen Olafsen, 69-84. London, United Kingdom: Palgrave Macmillan.

Klak, Thomas, James Wiley, Emma Gaalaas Mullaney, Swetha Peteru, Seann Regan, and Jean-Yves Merilus. 2011. "Inclusive Neoliberalism? Perspectives from Eastern Caribbean Farmers." Progress in Development Studies 11 (1): 33-61.

Lewis, W. Arthur. 1954. "Economic Development with Unlimited Supplies of Labour." *The Manchester School* 22 (2): 139–191.

Lipsey, Richard, and Alec Chrystal. 2003. *Economics*. Oxford, United Kingdom: Oxford University Press.

Loh Rahim, Hardy, Mohd Ali Bahari Abdul Kadir, Zanariah Zainal Abidin, Junainah Junid, Laila Mohd Kamaruddin, Noor Faizah Mohd Lajin, Siti Zahrah Buyong, and Adlan Ahmad Bakri. 2015. "Entrepreneurship Education in Malaysia: A Critical Review." *Journal of Technology Management and Business* 2 (2): 1-11.

LTT (Laws of Trinidad and Tobago). 1976. "The Constitution of the Republic of Trinidad and Tobago. Amended by Act 89 of 2000." Accessed October 12, 2019.
https://www.oas.org/juridico/english/mesicic3_tto_constitution.pdf

McLean, Sheldon, and Don Charles. 2018. "A Global Value Chain Analysis of Offshore Medical Universities in the Caribbean." *ECLAC Studies and Perspectives* 69: 1-44.

Mhango, Baijah. 1991. The Political Economy of Aid: The Case of Suriname." *Caribbean Studies* 24 (1/2): 123-164.

Nawaz, Waqas, and Muammer Koç. 2020. *Industry, University and Government Partnerships for the Sustainable Development of Knowledge-Based Society: Drivers, Models and Examples in US, Norway, Singapore and Qatar*. Cham, Switzerland: Springer Nature.

Nawawi, Atiqah, Narina A. Samah, Sharifah Osman and Hadijah Jaffri. 2020. "The Practice of Entrepreneurship Education in a Malaysian Higher Education Institution: A Single Case Study." *International Journal of Psychosocial Rehabilitation* 24 (05): 188-195.

NEDCO (National Entrepreneurship Development Company Limited). 2015. "Thinking of Starting Your OWN Business?" Accessed December 26, 2019. http://www.culture.gov.tt/wp-content/uploads/2015/08/NEDCO-Products-Services-08.08.15.pdf

Ng, Raymond Keng Wan. 2015. "An Empirical Analysis of the Singapore Entrepreneurship Ecosystem: A Case Study for BRIC Economies to Ponder." In *Entrepreneurial Ecosystem*, edited by Mathew J ManimalaKishinchand Poornima Wasdani, 57-89. New Delhi, India: Springer India.

Nwekeaku, Charlie. 2013. "Entrepreneurship Education and Challenges to Nigerian Universities." *Journal of Education and Practice* 4 (3): 1-6.

Obaji, Nkem Okpa, Chikodi Onyemerela, and Mercy Uche Olugu. 2015. "Entrepreneurship and Business Incubation Programme: The Sure Couple." *International Journal of Science, Technology and Management* 04 (01): 2394-9.

Obeleagu-Nzelibe, C. G., and R. K. Moruku. 2010. "Entrepreneurship and Economic Development: The Imperative for Curriculum Innovation in Nigerian Universities." Faculty of Administration, Nasarawa State University, Keffi, Nigeria Conference Proceeding.

Palmigiani, Fabio. 2022. "Guyana Approves Landmark Local Content Law for Oil Projects." Accessed February 7, 2022. https://www.upstreamonline.com/politics/guyana-approves-landmark-local-content-law-for-oil-projects/2-1-1138222

Parolini, Antonella, and Cindy Platek. 2010. "Offshore Medical Schools in the Caribbean." Accessed November 10, 2015. https://wenr.wes.org/2010/06/wenr-june-2010-feature

Patel, Trushar, and Premal Soni. 2013. "E-commerce in Developing Countries." *Oriental Journal of Computer Science & Technology* 6(3): 357-361.

Patterson, Eliza. 2001. "The US-EU Banana Dispute." Accessed April 5, 2019. https://www.asil.org/insights/volume/6/issue/4/us-eu-banana-dispute

Paul, Anna-Lisa. 2016. "Education Minister: No Job Cuts at the Ministry." *Trinidad and Tobago Guardian,* July 15. http://www.guardian.co.tt/article-6.2.356067.4da9a5531f

—. 2019. "OJT Programme Oversubscribed. Pressure for Job Seekers." *Trinidad and Tobago Guardian,* March 16. http://www.guardian.co.tt/news/pressure-for-job-seekers-6.2.802639.29f29a9af6

Perron, Pierre. 1997. "Further Evidence on Breaking Trend Functions in Macroeconomic Variables." *Journal of Econometrics* 80 (2): 355-385.

Poten and Partners. 2015. "Trinidad and Tobago Gas Master Plan." Accessed June 14, 2017. https://www.dropbox.com/s/lp3pjgpb6tiussp/Trinidad%20and%20Tobago%20Gas%20Master%20Plan.pdf?dl=0&fbclid=IwAR0dkcelZ5tknbSXMPHXlGtI7j2m7nmyrTx2i_XEheCTef6tvxalMcKTQpA

PRTT (Parliament of the Republic of Trinidad and Tobago). 2012. "Tackling Youth Unemployment in Trinidad and Tobago and the Caribbean." Accessed October 30, 2019. http://www.cpahq.org/cpahq/cpadocs/Wade-Paper%20on%20Tackling%20Youth%20Unemployment_58th%20CPC.pdf

—. 2018. "Joint Select Committee on Social Services and Public Administration." Accessed November 4, 2019. http://www.ttparliament.org/documents/news/mr337DC9.PDF

PSC (Public Service Commission). 2016. "Public Service Commission 2016 Annual Report." Accessed November 3, 2019. http://scd.org.tt/images/annual_reports/PSC_Annual_Reports/PSC%202016%20Annual%20Report.pdf

Ramsoedh, Hans. 2016. "Democracy and political culture in Suriname." In *Post-Colonial Trajectories in the Caribbean: The Three Guianas*, edited by Rosemarijn Hoefte, Matthew L. Bishop, Peter Clegg, 30-45. London, United Kingdom: Routledge.

Romer, Paul M. 1986. "Increasing Returns and Long-Run Growth." *Journal of Political Economy* 94 (5): 1002-1037.

Schumpeter, Joseph A. 1911. *The Theory of Economic Development.* Cambridge, MA, United States: Harvard University Press.

Shah, Raffique. 2016. "Sugar Industry Was Doomed to Fail: The Truth Behind Caroni's Closure." *Wired,* July 26. Accessed October 31, 2019. https://wired868.com/2016/07/26/sugar-industry-was-doomed-to-fail-the-truth-behind-caronis-closure/

Simms, Errol, Ruby Alleyne, Teresa Davidson, Nievel Niles-Rolingson, Gaynelle Holdip, Beverly Khan, Susan Smith-Bailey, Rolph Balgobin, and Richard Saunders. 2016. "Report of the GATE Task Force." Accessed October 29, 2019. http://parlcloud.ttparliament.org:8081/PapersLaidViewer/TempFiles/Report%20of%20the%20GATE%20Task%20Force.pdf

Singh, Nadaleen. 2013. "Business incubator programme spends $16m in 18 months." *Trinidad and Tobago Guardian*, May 15. Accessed December 26, 2019. https://www.guardian.co.tt/article-6.2.401046.3d8934cc41

Stevenson, Howard H. 1983. *A Perspective on Entrepreneurship*. Vol. 13. Cambridge, MA: Harvard Business School.

Sutton, Paul. 2006. *Modernizing the State: Public Sector Reform in the Commonwealth Caribbean*. Kingston, Jamaica: Ian Randle Publishers.

Tabbron, Geoffrey, and Jin Yang. 1997. "The Interaction Between Technical and Vocational Education and Training (TVET) and Economic Development in Advanced Countries." *International Journal of Educational Development* 17 (3): 323-334.

Thomas, Clive Y. 2020. "Guyana and the Advent of World-Class Petroleum Finds." *Handbook of Caribbean Economies*: 289-303.

Tope, Alabi, Alanana Osana Otaki, and Bahal Margret. 2014. "Entrepreneurship Education: A Panacea to Graduate Unemployment in Nigeria." *Journal of Sustainable Development in Africa* 16 (3): 1-9.

Trinidad and Tobago Newsday. 2019. "The New NEDCO Business Accelerator." Accessed December 26, 2019. https://newsday.co.tt/2019/12/22/the-new-nedco-business-accelerator/

TTconnect. 2019. "General Information." Accessed October 25, 2019. https://www.ttconnect.gov.tt/gortt/portal/ttconnect/!ut/p/a1/jdDBCoJAEAbgp_

UWI (University of the West Indies). 2019. "Estimated 9,300 to Receive Degrees at 2019 UWI Graduations." Accessed October 29, 2019. https://sta.uwi.edu/news/releases/release.asp?id=21981

van Dijck, Pitou, Geske Dijkstra, Niek de Jong, Dougal Martin, and Rob Vos. 2000. "The Suriname Economy: Experiences of the 1990s and Challenges Ahead." Working Paper, Centre for Latin American Research and Documentation (CEDLA), University of Amsterdam, Hague, the Netherlands.

VanGrasstek, Craig. 2013. *The History and Future of the World Trade Organisation*. Geneva: World Trade Organisation.

Vos, Rob, Niek de Jong, and Geske Dijkstra. 1999. "Employment, Poverty and Income Distribution in Suriname in the 1990s." Accessed December 3, 2021.
researchgate.net/profile/Rob-Vos/publication/264165632_Employment_Poverty_and_Income_Distribution/

Wang, Fei. 2017. "Canadian Offshore Schools in China: A Comparative Policy Analysis." *Journal of Education Policy* 32(5), 523–541.

Weissman, Robert. 1990. "Playing with Numbers: The IMF's Fraud in Trinidad and Tobago." *The Multinational Monitor* 11 (6):1-10.

WITS (World Integrated Trade Solution). 2019. "Trade Data (UN Comtrade)." Accessed November 12, 2019.
http://wits.worldbank.org/WITS/WITS/AdvanceQuery/RawTradeData/QueryDefinition.aspx?Page=RawTradeData

Wolff, Laurence. 2009. "Challenges and Opportunities for Postsecondary Education and Training in Barbados, Bahamas, Guyana, Jamaica, and Trinidad & Tobago." In *Community College Models,* edited by Rosalind Latiner Raby, Edward J. Valeau, 173-195. Switzerland: Springer.

World Bank. 2021. "Data." Accessed December 29, 2021.
https://data.worldbank.org/

Wrana, Jöran, and Thi Xuan Thu Nguyen. 2019. "Strategic Coupling and Regional Development in a Transition Economy: What Can We Learn from Vietnam?" *Area Development and Policy*: 1-12.

Zhou, Ping. 2019. "The History of Singapore's Economic Development." Accessed December 13, 2021. https://www.thoughtco.com/singapores-economic-development-1434565

APPENDIX

A.0 Econometric (Empirical) Analysis of the Statistical impact of Services Upon Economic Output

A.1 Data

The variables considered for analysis are Real Per Capita GDP Growth (GDP), Services Growth (SER), and Manufacturing Value Added Growth (MAN). Data on T&T's Real Per Capita GDP is obtained from the World Bank online database.[42] From such data, the growth was computed as the percentage change in the GDP. This data was available over the 1980 to 2020 period.

Services data was obtained from the United Nations Conference on Trade and Development (UNCTAD) Statistical database.[43] There was services data for T&T for the BPMP5 classification over the 1980 to the 2011 period. There was also services data for T&T for the BPM6 classification over the 2005 to 2020 period. The growth was computed as the percentage change in services. Although there is a difference in the BPM5 and BPM6 classifications, there were minor differences in the growth rates for the years where the 2 classifications overlapped (2006-2010). Subsequently, the hot and cold imputation method was used to fill in the missing data. Thus, the growth rates of the BPM6 classification from 2011 to 2020 was added to the growth rates of the BPM5 classification over the period 1980 to 2010.

Manufacturing Value Added growth data was obtained from the World Bank database.[44] This data was available over the 1985 to 2019 period. An Autoregressive Moving Average (ARMA) (1,1) was used to perform a 1 step ahead out of sample forecast for the observation for 2020.

---

[42] The Source: https://data.worldbank.org/indicator/NY.GDP.PCAP.KD
[43] Source: http://unctadstat.unctad.org/wds/ReportFolders/reportFolders.aspx
[44] Source: https://data.worldbank.org/indicator/NV.IND.MANF.KD.ZG?locations=TT&view=chart

Since all data must have the same frequency and cover the same period to time to allow for time series analysis and regression, annual data over the 1985 to 2020 period was used for all variables. This time period produced 35 observations per variable.

A.2 Methodology: Pretesting

Before performing any analysis, several pretests were performed. Time series are noted to possess structural breaks.

The Chow Test for Structural Breaks allows for the testing of a structural break at a known break date. If there is a structural break at a particular point, separate regressions on subsamples created by the break date would produce a better model than a linear regression which covers the entire interval. Thus, the Chow Test uses an F-test to determine whether a single regression is more efficient than two separate regressions performed on two sub-samples of the data.

In the first case a single regression is used to fit the data points:

$$y_t = \alpha_0 + \alpha_t x_t + \varepsilon_t \quad (01)$$

In the second case, to test for the structural break, two linear regressions are performed on each sub-sample of the data

$$y_t = \beta_0 + \beta_{1t} x_t + \varepsilon_t \quad (02)$$

$$y_t = \delta_0 + \delta_{1t} x_t + \varepsilon_t \quad (03)$$

In the second case, if $\beta_0 = \delta_0$, $\beta_{1t} = \delta_{1t}$, then models 2 and 3 can be expressed as a single model. The F-statistic which uses the residual sum of squares (RSS) to test the parameters for equivalence is given by

$$F = \frac{RSS_1 - (RSS_2 + RSS_3)/k}{RSS_2 + RSS_3/n - 2k} \quad (04)$$

Bai and Perron (1998) L+1 versus L breakpoints test begins with a linear regression with all the regressors, then finds potential breakpoints by global minimization of the sum-of-squared residuals. At each subsample with a breakpoint, a test of parameter constancy is applied. The test starts with a null hypothesis of L = 0 breaks vs an alternative hypothesis of L+1 =1 break. If the null hypothesis is rejected, the test proceeds with a null hypothesis of L=1 break vs an alternative hypothesis of L+1=2 breaks. This pattern continues until the number of structural breaks is identified.

After the application of the structural break test, each time series is tested for weak sense stationarity. A stationary time series is one whose first and second-order moment conditions of mean, variance, and covariance are all constant over time. Stationarity is a useful property in time series analysis, since if the mean and variance is constant over time, the parameters of the time series could be reliably predicted over time.

The Augmented Dickey Fuller (ADF) test, the Phillips Perron (PP) test, the Kwiatkowski–Phillips–Schmidt–Shin (KPSS) test, and the Perron (1989) breakpoint test are used to investigate the stationarity of the time series. The null hypothesis of the aforementioned stationarity test is the presence of a unit root in the time series ($H_0: \rho = 1$) , vs an alternative hypothesis of less than 1 unit root ($H_1: \rho < 1$).

Note, in a simple autoregressive process: $y_t = \rho y_{t-1} + x_t^{'}\delta + \varepsilon_t$, if $|\rho| \geq 1$, then y is non-stationary.

If the time series appears to be non-stationary, the next step involves the testing for cointegration. Cointegration is the presence of a long-run statistical relationship between time series. Two time series may be non-stationary and I(1), however, a linear regression of the two time series may produce a residual which is stationary and I(0). This suggests that in the short-run the two time series may drift apart, but there is a causal relationship existing between the two time series and in the long run they converge to that relationship.

Since three rather than two variables are under consideration, the Johansen (1995) Test is used to test for cointegration. Consider a Vector Autoregression (VAR)[45] of order p

$$y_t = \beta_1 y_{t-1} + \cdots + \beta_p y_{t-p} + Bx_t + \varepsilon_t \quad (05)$$

where y_t represents a k x 1 column vector of non-stationary dependent variables, x_t is a k x 1 column vector of deterministic variables, β_p represents the k x p matrix of estimated parameters for lagged variables, and ε_t is the column vector with the error term.

The VAR may also be expressed as

[45] A VAR is a system with m variables, each of which is expressed as a linear function of p lags of itself and of all of the other $m - 1$ variables, plus an error term.

$$\Delta y_t = \Pi y_{t-1} + \sum_{i=1}^{p-1} \Gamma_i \, \Delta y_{t-i} + Bx_t + \varepsilon_t \tag{06}$$

where

$$\Pi = \sum_{i=1}^{p-1} \mathrm{A}_i - I, \text{ and } \Gamma_i = -\sum_{j=i+1}^{p} A_j \tag{07}$$

If the coefficient matrix Π has a reduced where $r < k$, (the number of columns (r) is less than the number of rows (k)) then there exist k x r matrices α and β each with rank r, such that $\Pi = \alpha\beta'$ and $\beta' y_t$ are both stationary and I(0). r is also the number of cointegrating columns in matrix β. It is noteworthy that the rank of matrix β will also be the number of cointegrating columns of matrix β. Thus, the Johansen method computes the matrix Π, and determines the number of linearly independent columns of matrix β to determine its rank and number of cointegrating column vectors.

A.3 Methodology: Regression

Once cointegration is found between the variables, the Vector Error Correction Model (VECM), which is an extension of the VAR model to account for cointegration, will be used. In a 3 variable system, a VECM may be represented by

$$\Delta y_{1t} = \beta_{01} + \sum_{i=1}^{p} \Delta \beta_{1p} y_{1t-p} + \sum_{i=1}^{p} \Delta \beta_{1p} x_{1t-p} + \sum_{i=1}^{p} \Delta \beta_{1p} g_{1t-p} - z_{1t} + \varepsilon_{1t} \tag{08}$$

$$\Delta x_{2t} = \beta_{02} + \sum_{i=1}^{p} \Delta \beta_{2p} y_{2t-p} + \sum_{i=1}^{p} \Delta \beta_{2p} x_{2t-p} + \sum_{i=1}^{p} \Delta \beta_{2p} g_{2t-p} + z_{2t} + \varepsilon_{2t} \tag{09}$$

$$\Delta g_t = \beta_{03} + \sum_{i=1}^{p} \Delta \beta_{3p} y_{3t-p} + \sum_{i=1}^{p} \Delta \beta_{3p} x_{3t-p} + \sum_{i=1}^{p} \Delta \beta_{3p} g_{3t-p} + z_{3t} + \varepsilon_{3t} \tag{10}$$

$$z_t = y_t - \beta_0 - \beta_1 x_t - \beta_2 g_t \tag{11}$$

where Δ represents the change in each variable, y_t, x_t, and $g_t$are the variables each of which is expressed as a linear function of p lags of itself and all of the other, each β_p represents an estimated parameter, Σ is the summation of the product of the variables and the parameters, z_{1t}, z_{2t}, and z_{3t} are the error-correction parameters that measure how y and x react to deviations from long-run equilibrium, and ε_t is the error term for each equation. Note, lags are not introduced for the error correction term as doing such would introduce the problem of perfect multicollinearity in the model.

The structure of Equations (08) to (10) models how the values of the variables in period *t* are related to past (*t-p*) values. Thus, the VECM forecasts the future paths of *x, y,* and *g* conditional on their past values.

It is noteworthy that the optimal lag length must be specified for any VECM used. An optimal lag length should be chosen, since if the lag order is unnecessarily large, the forecast precision of the corresponding VECM (p) would be reduced. In other words, if the wrong lag length of the VECM (p) is selected, the model becomes less accurate.

It is standard for the lag length of VARs and VECMs to be selected based on information criteria. The lag length that minimizes the value of information criteria (log-likelihood (logL), likelihood ratio (LR), Final Prediction Error Criterion (FPE), Akaike's Information Criterion (AIC), Schwarz Criterion (SC), Hannan-Quinn Criterion (HQ)) is typically used as the optimal lag length. Subsequently, the aforementioned information criteria are used to determine the VECM's optimal lag length.

A.4 Methodology: Diagnostic Testing

As a diagnostic test, the VECM must be tested for stability.

If a VECM is to be represented by Equations (08) to (11), then let F represent a 3 x p matrix of the estimated parameters for each variable. Then, the determinant finding the characteristic equation is

$$|F - \lambda I_{Np}| = (-1)^{Np}|\lambda^p I_N - \lambda^{p-1}\beta_1 - \cdots - \beta_p| = 0 \qquad (12)$$

where I is the identity matrix, β denotes the estimated parameters which are used to construct F, Np is the number of variables (3).

The stability condition of a VECM is that inverse roots of the characteristic equation must lie inside of the unit circle. The required condition is that the inverse roots of $|\boldsymbol{\beta(q)}| = \mathbf{0}$ must lie inside of the unit circle. This implies that the eigenvalues of $\boldsymbol{\beta_1}$ lie inside of the unit circle.

After confirming stability, another diagnostic is a test for serial correlation. The Portmanteau Serial Correlation Test can be applied.

The Portmanteau Serial Correlation Test computes the multivariate Box-Pierce/Ljung-Box Q-statistics for residual serial correlation up to the specified order. The null hypothesis of the Portmanteau Serial Correlation Test is there is no serial correlation up to lag h. This is tested against the alternative hypothesis of the presence of serial correlation at lag h. The test statistics are given by

$$Q_{BP} = n \sum_{k=1}^{m} \hat{r}_k^2 \tag{13}$$

$$Q_{LB} = n(n+2) \sum_{k=1}^{m} \frac{\hat{r}_k^2}{n-k} \tag{14}$$

where Equation (13) is the original Box-Pierce statistic, Equation (14) is the original Ljung-Box statistic, $\hat{r}_k$ is the sample autocorrelation of order k in the residual. Both statistics follow the chi-square (χ^2) distribution with (*m-p-q*) degrees of freedom.

VAR and VECM models are interpreted by the impulse response and variance decomposition functions. The impulse response traces the effect of a shock to the variable that is ordered first upon the other variables in the model. The Variance Decomposition tells how much of a change in a variable is due to its own shock and how much is due to shocks to other variables.

A.5 Results

To undertake structural break tests, first, a linear regression must be specified using OLS. The linear regression must not include any autoregressive or moving average terms. In the following exercise, the Real Per Capita GDP Growth (*GDP*) is specified as the dependent variable, and Services Growth (*SER*) and Manufacturing Value Added Growth (*MAN*) are specified as independent variables.

In the Chow test for structural breaks, the following break dates are considered 2000, 2008, 2010, and 2014. The null hypothesis of the Chow test is there are no breaks, and the alternative hypothesis is a structural break at a specific break date. As can be seen in Table A.01, the probability of the test statistic in the Chow test was 0.2455 and greater than the 10%, 5%, and 1% significance level, suggesting the non-rejection of the null hypothesis.

Table A.01: Chow Test

Chow Breakpoint Test: 2000 2008 2010 2014
Null Hypothesis: No breaks at specified breakpoints
Varying regressors: All equation variables
Equation Sample: 1985 2020

F-statistic	1.451113	Prob. F(8,26)	0.2230
Log likelihood ratio	13.28920	Prob. Chi-Square(8)	0.1023
Wald Statistic	11.60890	Prob. Chi-Square(8)	0.1695

In Bai-Perron tests of L+1 vs. L globally determined breaks, at each step it tests for l breaks vs an alternative of l + 1 breaks.

Table A.02: Bai-Perron Test of L+1 vs. L Globally Determined Breaks

Break Test	F-statistic	Scaled F-statistic	Critical Value**
0 vs. 1	4.828544	9.657087	11.47
1 vs. 2	2.651477	5.302954	12.95
2 vs. 3	0.691507	1.383014	14.03
3 vs. 4	0.537071	1.074141	14.85
4 vs. 5	0.519202	1.038403	15.29

In Table A.02, the test statistic of 4.82 is less than the critical value of 11.47. Given that the test is right-tailed, it suggested the non-rejection of the null hypothesis of 0 breaks in favour of the alternative hypothesis of 1 break. Thus, both the Chow Test and the Bai-Perron Test of L+1 vs. L Globally Determined Breaks tests suggest no structural breaks in the linear time series regression.

Next, the time series are tested for stationarity.

Table A.03: Stationarity Tests

	GDP	SER	MAN
ADF	0.1169 (level) 0000 (1st diff)	0.0013 (level)	0.0000 (level) 0000 (1st diff)
PP	0.1754 (level) 0.0000 (1st diff)	0.0014 (level)	0.0001 (level) 0000 (1st diff)
KPSS	0.221400	0.298452	0.182376
Perron (1998)	0.2973	0.01	0.01

KPSS critical values

1% level	0.739000
5% level	0.463000
10% level	0.347000

The null hypothesis of the KPSS test is that the time series is stationary (has 0 unit roots), the alternative hypothesis is that the time series is non-stationary (has at least 1 unit root). The KPSS test is also a right-tailed test. Since the value of the KPSS statistic for each variable was less than the critical values, it suggested the non-rejection of the null hypothesis.
The null hypothesis of the Perron (1998) break point test is that the time series has a unit root (non-stationary) with a structural break.

The ADF, the PP, and Perron (1998) tests suggest that the GDP growth is non-stationary, but services growth, and manufacturing growth were stationary. Given the difference in order of integration the variables were tested for cointegration (long-run relationship) within a block.

Table A.04: Johansen Cointegration Test

Hypothesized No. of CE(s)	Eigenvalue	Trace Statistic	0.05 Critical Value	Prob.**
None *	0.418382	36.62848	29.79707	0.0070
At most 1 *	0.382326	18.74440	15.49471	0.0156
At most 2	0.082606	2.845186	3.841466	0.0916

As can be seen in Table A.04: The null hypothesis of at most 2 cointegrating vectors was not rejected since the probability of the test statistic was 0.0916 and greater than the 0.05% significance level. This suggested the existence of cointegration between the variables. Thus, the Vector Error Correction Model (VECM) is used for the modelling framework since it can take into consideration the long-run (cointegrating) relationship between the variables within a system.

Table A.05: Lag Length Test

Lag	LogL	LR	FPE	AIC	SC	HQ
0	-353.6430	NA	489505.7	21.61473	21.75077*	21.66050*
1	-342.9827	18.73624*	444216.1*	21.51410*	22.05829	21.69721
2	-334.6611	13.11279	470339.8	21.55522	22.50754	21.87565

Before the specification of the VECM, a lag length test is performed to determine the optimal number of lags. In Table A.05, 3 out of 6 information criteria suggest that 1 lag is the optimal number of lags. Thus, 1 lag is used in the VECM.

Note: In this test, the optimal lag will be the one with the smallest values for the information criterion.

Table A.06: VECM

Cointegrating Eq:	CointEq1		
GDP(-1)	1.000000		
SER(-1)	-0.196425 (0.05790) [-3.39248]		
MAN(-1)	-0.723766 (0.09518) [-7.60433]		
C	0.562652		
Error Correction:	D(GDP)	D(SER)	D(MAN)
CointEq1	-0.164248 (0.17842) [-0.92056]	0.500917 (0.85500) [0.58587]	1.711440 (0.32501) [5.26580]
D(GDP(-1))	-0.374116 (0.18504) [-2.02182]	-0.177871 (0.88671) [-0.20060]	-0.346881 (0.33707) [-1.02912]
D(SER(-1))	0.016498 (0.04305) [0.38325]	-0.358381 (0.20628) [-1.73733]	0.310877 (0.07841) [3.96454]
D(MAN(-1))	-0.021544 (0.08530) [-0.25256]	0.237741 (0.40877) [0.58161]	0.193387 (0.15538) [1.24457]
C	-0.087931 (0.74893) [-0.11741]	-1.360559 (3.58888) [-0.37910]	-0.484920 (1.36424) [-0.35545]
R-squared	0.225218	0.173772	0.625534
Adj. R-squared	0.118352	0.059810	0.573884

In Table A.06, it is noteworthy that the coefficient of the first cointegrating equation is negative, while the remaining cointegrating equations are positive.

VARs and VECMs should not be interpreted via the coefficients estimated in the system. They should be analysed by the impulse response and variance decompositions. However, before proceeding to such analysis, diagnostic tests are performed.

The VECM is tested for stability.

Figure A.01: VECM stability test

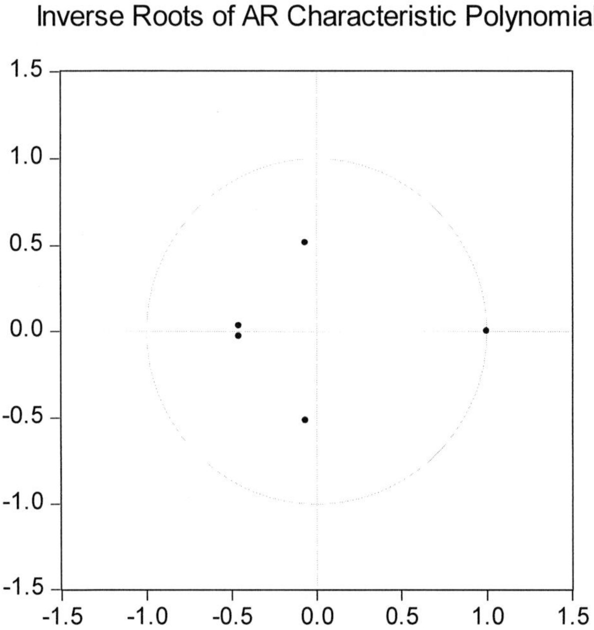

As can be seen in Figure A.01, the inverse roots of the autoregressive characteristic polynomial all lie within the unit circle. This suggests that the VECM is stable. Note, 1 inverse root is on the circumference of the unit circle because the VECM was non-stationary at level.

Next, the Portmanteau Test is performed for serial correlation.

Table A.07: Portmanteau Serial Correlation Test

VEC Residual Portmanteau Tests for Autocorrelations
Null Hypothesis: no residual autocorrelations up to lag h
Date: 01/22/22 Time: 18:37
Sample: 1985 2020
Included observations: 34

Lags	Q-Stat	Prob.	Adj Q-Stat	Prob.	df
1	2.308029	NA*	2.377970	NA*	NA*
2	10.78497	0.7677	11.38472	0.7249	15

As can be seen in Table A.07, the probability of the test statistic at 2 lags is 0.7249 and greater than the 10% level of significance, suggesting the non-rejection of the null hypothesis of no-serial correlation.

Given the favourable results, the impulse response and variance decompositions are estimated.

Figure A.02: Impulse Response

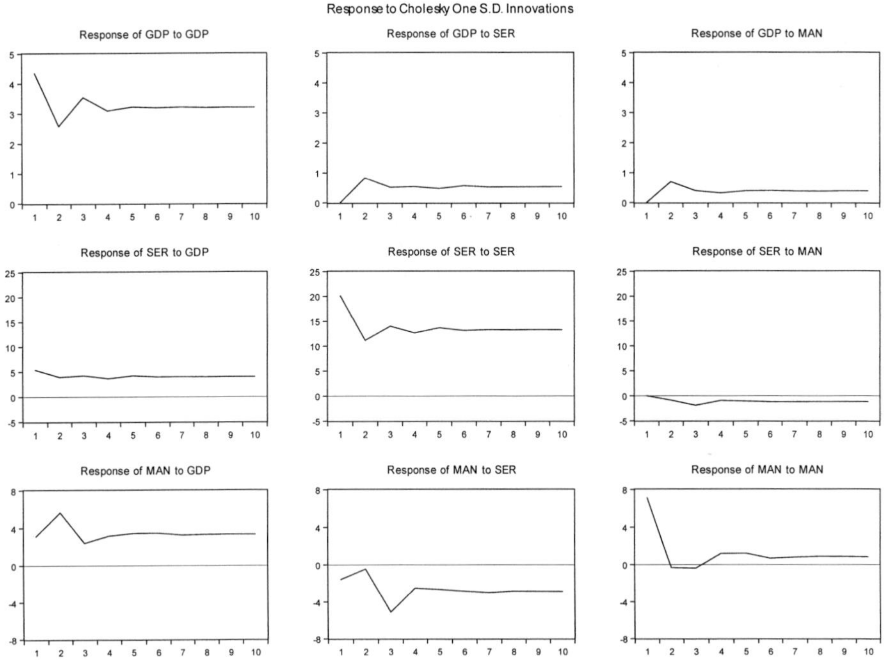

Table A.08: Variance Decomposition Results of Per Capita GDP

Period	S.E.	GDP	SER	MAN
1	20.86762	6.669484	**93.33052**	0.000000
2	24.00062	7.741079	**92.12192**	0.137004
3	28.15734	7.879738	**91.56023**	0.560036
4	31.09727	7.851554	**91.59027**	0.558171
5	34.24043	7.960350	**91.47661**	0.563043
6	36.90722	8.017549	**91.39231**	0.590137
7	39.44822	8.054515	**91.33340**	0.612089
8	41.81718	8.077730	**91.30090**	0.621369
9	44.07532	8.103646	**91.26595**	0.630406
10	46.21347	8.122566	**91.23855**	0.638882

Table A.08 displays the results of the variance decomposition.

In the VECM model, the GDP growth (GDP) was ordered first, then services (SER), then manufacturing (MAN). This was done to allow the shock to go to GDP growth first as it is the main variable of interest. Then the shock is allowed to go to services, then to manufacturing. The key relationship of interest is the impact of services on per capita GDP. This can be determined from the variance decomposition of services on GDP.

The variance decomposition suggests that after a 1 standard deviation shock in the initial period, services contributed 92% to GDP in the 2nd period. Services contribution slightly decreased to 91% to GDP in the 3rd period. In contrast, the variance decomposition for manufacturing suggested that it would contribute 0.13% to GDP in the 2nd period, and 0.56% in the 3rd period. Although these results are from an econometric model and not actual performance, the results suggest **that services may have a greater contribution to T&T's economy than manufacturing.** If these results are accurate, then it would be logical for the GORTT to focus its effort on enhancing the services sector as it generates a significant contribution to T&T's economy.